P174 Satisfy yourself first. know ↙!

P.101. Only to the The magician is the world for ever fluid

P 49   Adorning oneself

P 47   What shape experience

P188   Tuning fork

P 238
LAST 3 #'s
All 239

P
1778 Trait!
Art Museum
rule

How to tell a story

Writing Open the Mind

Writing Open the Mind

Tapping the Subconscious to
Free the Writing and the Writer

ANDY COUTURIER

Ulysses Press

Quotes on pages 25, 79, 80, and 83 originally appeared in *The Practice of the Wild* by Gary Snyder, Shoemaker & Hoard, Emeryville, CA: 1990. We thank Avalon Publishing Group, Inc., for permission to reprint these.

Published by: Ulysses Press
P.O. Box 3440
Berkeley, CA 94703
www.ulyssespress.com

Library of Congress Control Number: 2005922425
ISBN: 1-56975-476-4

Printed in Canada by Transcontinental Printing

10 9 8 7 6 5 4 3 2 1

Editor: Lynette Ubois
Acquisition Editor: Ashley Chase
Editorial and production staff: Matt Orendorff, Lisa Kester,
    Tamara Kowalski
Cover design: Leslie Henriques
Cover illustration: Kevin Tolman/Photodisc Green/Getty Images
Illustrations on page 230: Greg Couturier
Photo on page 244: John Gibler

Distributed by Publishers Group West

To Cynthia,
who knew what to do.

Table of Contents

Pre-Amble

Could you be open to the proposition that the murky and quirky part of your mind is wiser than the thrust-and-parry date-book mind? Here we have discovery by means of imagination. No need to grip the steering wheel so tight. Enjoyment is what it's all about. Let go. The mind likes that. It responds well to indulgence.

People talk about "freewriting." Free. Writing. What would it be to write totally free? To be liberated from all the niggling habits, the tendency to adopt a certain stance, the preference for the word "mitigating" over the word "*Shazam!*"? What might your mind do and say if it weren't in the office drafting memos? A sassafras hallelujah hickey zowie brainstorm.

Writing discovers your own life. Don't box it. Don't expect it or force it to be this or that. The way most of us approach writing, we're stuck in the detention room. "Is this incoherent?" we ask the poor beleaguered mind. "Is it choppy, is it vague?" "Will Mrs. Mergatroid attack it with a red pen?" We boss it around: "A beginning, middle, and end!" "Be objective!" "Don't use the passive voice." And the poor mind: "Help! I can't move!"

But when we give ourselves permission to play with our writing, the subconscious is liberated and it makes patterns outside of the analyzing mind, outside of the Self-Other mind. And those patterns are far more complex and rich (as is the logic of dreams), than a strict Euclidean geometry that has been cleansed of all the burrs, rough edges, tangled mats of hair, and seaweed clumps. That richness can be felt and sensed. Watch it with your blinking eyes as your writings change through the book.

For, you see, writing is understanding what you already know, as well as discovering what you didn't know, as well as intoxicatingly stumbling upon what you didn't know you knew. Think of this book as a delicious compendium of tricks, stratagems, and experiments to let you into your own subconscious world. You conjure up a particular state of consciousness, and let the words *emit* from that place.

Tricks! They're never the same twice.

So here are some hints and clues for our journey: Follow that wisp of smoke emanating from the forest. "What's *happening* in there?" Second, be kind to the self. Be generous and do not evaluate. Sweetness is good. Third, *Relaaax*! This is your time: an unhurried time. These gateways to the subconscious work when you remain open and watching and delighted. Let us be interested in the New. Inexplicable. Bonk!

We'll be experimenting here with following a train of thought as well as breaking it, or baffling it. We'll try a scrambling or shuffling of a piece you have already written, or getting ourselves hypnotized with incense smoke, or place, or mystical images, or light, or the haunted sounds on an old haunted house LP and writing from there. We'll use rhythm and repetition, the sensuous world of Nature, and the clottings and slitherings of word textures too. At the end you'll start to make up maneuvers and trumps yourself. As they used to say about the Internet (except this time it's true): "The possibilities are *endless*."

**Use the mind to bend the words,
and the words to bend the mind**

The child is full of play. What stilts us and stops us from play? Well, *fear*, for one. If you say to yourself, "Is this bad? Is this what they want? What if that's a cliché?" If you say this to yourself as you're forming letters, what will that writing sound like? How will *you* feel writing it? If you clench around your writing, it'll come out clenched, like a neurotic crimp-necked chimp . . . if it comes out at all. But if you say to yourself, "Good! Fun! Why not? Try this! Go to town! Freak out!" *then* what will the writing sound like?

So what are the toxins of writing? One: Competition. What we are doing here in this book is not about "better" or who is "a writer." Who wants all that bogus me-versus-you? Find out what your squirmy self wants to write, or your dreamy self, or your puckish self. Turn off the calibrator. Two: Shackling ourselves to the proper and correct topic to write about. Here you can write about anything you want. Could be mundane, could be scary, could be nonsense. Lewd or illegal. Writing is a free place. Always seek your own pleasure and enjoyment. Three: Doing it the right way. There is no right way. Nothing in the subconscious is about correctness, or even about sentences. Your mind can only discover freedom when you let it be its own juju, kabalistic, honky-tonk, Romper Room way.

the spacious
specious
capacious
capricious
writer

Do everything you want and nothing you don't.

And don't forget to pursue a wellness in writing. Serious business! Ernest Hemingway, Hunter S. Thompson, Sylvia Plath. Writers are offing themselves because of the suffering. But writing misery is, like, so 20th Century! Don't go there. "A rejection of miserablism," say the surrealists. Always take care of yourself. Be well.

Now, you can tell already that your friend Andy likes to populate sentences with wacko zombie and exclamation points. But (I am propounding) the world has gotten altogether too stuffy. Enthusiasm has been punctured, debased. Pleasure in writing is taboo. Roland Barthes wisely spoke thus, "Pleasure is continually disappointed, reduced, defeated, in favor of strong, noble values: Truth, Death, Progress, Struggle, etc."

And even though I love to goof around a lot and joke and all, there is something serious here. My bestest friend in the whole world Cynthia said, "There are all these forces these days that prevent us from listening to what's going on inside: consumerism, the media, street noise, the age of the expert." And she's right. People have been told that what they say doesn't matter, that the way or style or "skill" they say it with is more important, and should be judged. They've also been told that they can get better at writing by doing certain right things. In other words, fit into a mold. Crank it out at the cookie-cutter factory.

But they have never been told that language comes from the deep wilderness of life itself. That it comes from and through play, that it resonates in the body, the physical body, that it indeed changes the body as it is made, and that it is swayed by light and sound and the room that you are in. They've been made to separate writing and pleasure. And that is Bad.

People write because they need to. People make stories for themselves and others, to fight the bomb, or the war, or to fix the broken places. We electric socket into the full power of our Selves by scribbling into our interior hinterlands.

That's why we do not dislike one kind of writing or another. It's not nice. One of the main mantras here is, "No disparaged forms of writing!" These ruses work no matter what kind of writing you do. You can access the subliminal mind for writing cover letters, or pissed-off tirades against racism, or prayers, or for figuring out why she said that to you. So let us put aside for the moment those standard classifications of poetry, fiction, non-fiction, and "just" journal writing. (In any case, they flow into each other.) And will I go even more anarchist commune than that, and state that it is Not True that only some kinds of writing are "creative writing." What we want is beyond those boxy boxes.

Now in this world there are many writing books chock full of topics on which to write. Here's an excellent one, "Where do things come from and where do they go?" Let us clink to the red wine of great writing topics. And although I've scattered fun examples like that throughout, this is not a book full of subjects to write on. I leave it up to the World to appeal to you.

This book is, instead, a compilation of wheels and pulleys and chutes and ladders to plug your topic into. And it's also more than that. It's a free zone, really, where freedom itself is examined, and you create your *own* chutes and ladders, and learn how to make them out of manila envelopes and pillboxes and soda cans, and then run them topics or stories or poems through the hamster wheel of your own consciousness. That's why these are more *experiments* than exercises. An exercise has a set goal in mind that the person giving you the exercise wants you to get. Like a nautilus machine or something. This book doesn't want some specific thing from you. It's up to you to want things from you. An experiment is about finding out What will happen? It's about opening, and being curious.

One suggestion for you while you are going about this "subconscious" business: what you write may sometimes feel like utter chaos and nonsense when you're in the middle of it (and that's why the literal mind doesn't understand it), but just *keep moving the pen*, because what you want is to stumble upon something unexpected. (Which is why I can't tell you what's going to happen to you in this book. If I could, then it would be pre-predicted, and that would be the opposite of you being free.)

Now a couple of things about this book's structure. I've grouped together these tricks, cajolings, and entrancements in different sets of "Openings" (just to be conventional, we can call them "chapters") such as Shatter/Scramble and Sway and Subliminal Realms, according to what type of elastic properties they have on the mind. And each of the experiments within them, each of these Gateways to the Subconscious, is structured like this:

- An induction into what we will do.
- "Try it!": The technique itself.
- "Questions for the Curious": An inquiry into the mind of the writer—the writer being you.
- "The Mind of It": My thinkings about what this technique does and why it does it (so-called "learned commentary").

In each experiment, we might be writing with some topic you've chosen, but sometimes we will be just forming letters and words on the page with no topic at all, solely to discover what occurs without any intention at all. In some experiments we'll start something new and fresh, and other times we'll abscond with something you wrote yesterday, or ten years ago, or steal something from the newspaper and distort it entirely out of recognition. And why not? Text is infinitely mutatious: to pronounce something as forever done is to not be free. Let's not be not free.

And since this is all about finding the pleasure of writing, of course you should write with the pen and kind of paper that you totally love. Anything! Glass-tipped fountain pens on ragwool parchment, or stubby black crayons on torn paper bags. Find your own inimitable device. Do everything you want and nothing you don't.

But before we get started—I almost forgot!—what is the point of all of this freewriting? Well . . . wouldn't it be relaxing to just have a break from all this "point" stuff? Let's just let go of that for a while and find out what happens when you write this way.

You are your own mad scientist; you are your own sage.

A Tasting of Techniques: Experiments to Get You Started

Let's taste. Lying before you is a whole pandemonium of sideshow booths and three ring wing-ding extravaganzas. They are good.

In this first chutney of techniques, I'll lay out a few hors-d'oeuvres that you can fiddle with and explore and see what happens. One will be juxtaposing chunks, another will be snatching glimpses from the fog. We'll sheep dip into intuitive listing and shape shift from one fun house mirror to another. It'll be a kaleidoscope full of parakeets, a regular disco ball of Truth. And some other stuff too. What is "true" may shift under you, become fluid. Things that seemed chinked together in a particular way, immutable, can scratch and shift into an entirely other combobulation in a wink.

How exactly do things change in the mind? Let us just watch as we perform these presto change-os, and see what happens when we do. Let the focus shift: it will. The word to remember is "emit." Let your writing emit from the mindstate these techniques take you to. You don't need to force anything out. You don't need that much-ballyhooed triumph of the will. Instead we play, googly-eyed, with the pop rocks of syllables in the mouth

> Jumble scramble stumble tone! Use the language to get beyond the known.

and we do-si-do huge chunks of writing left and right that cat's-cradle into a new configuration of . . . Of what? Well that's what we don't yet know.

TECHNIQUE THE FIRST
Cobblings

The first liberation is of listing. Writing a list, there's nothing you can do wrong. The fact of the list asks you to add to it: it's an endless cabinet of blank spaces. Items can be crossed off with abandon, and new ones added. I like to think of a huge old abandoned post office in some Rust Belt city, and there you are, on the clerk side of all those P.O. boxes, thousands of them, each of them empty and ready to be filled. That's what a list can be. Because the slot is there, it asks to be filled.

Also! Lists can be re-ordered. They don't have a set sequence. And that means that each part is free to associate with other parts. A free association. Or dissociation. Words can gravitate toward each other. And they do.

TRY IT!

Choose something you've been wanting to write about. Anything is good. Surgery. Archery. Despair. The role of silver mining in the colonial economy of 18th century Mexico. Cliques in high school. Global warming. Anything at all. You've got things you want to write about.

Now take a wide sheet of paper and at the top write a phrase or a word to put that topic in ink on page. Some people like to call this a title. That's fine.

Under that, now, write five column headings. We're going to be playing here with abundance—plenty, lots. The headings are: "Scenes," "Moods," "Questions," "Concepts," "Faces." Scenes are places. Moods are feelings. Questions—you could name this column "Mysteries" if you prefer—are things you still don't know. (Not knowing is interesting, and just because we don't know, we don't have to turn away.) Concepts are ideas, thoughts you have about this. And faces, well, they're people, people associated with this topic, and you can see their faces.

So it looks like this:

| Scenes | Moods | Questions | Concepts | Faces |

Now take about seven vamping minutes and write down every single association or connection you have in your brain about said Topic, and fill up all of these columns. You will not be held accountable for using or even explaining all your list items, so just put down whatever you maybe might think you could use. This is because plenty is good, and because not stopping the pen tells the mind that the pen doesn't stop. (Telling the mind this has many beneficial by-products and rebates and waivers and tailfins and soda crackers.)

Also! You don't need to fill a single column first, all orderly-like, and then proceed diligently on to the next column. Jump all over the place. Let the question, "Why *does* she act like that?" lead, inexplicably, to the concept "trust," which engenders, then, in rapid succession, "doubt," "lies," "pancake batter" "frangipani," "my second-cousin's messy car" and "Bob Hope."

The pancake batter doesn't have a column! Dang! OK, then make a new column "Objects," or just call pancake batter a Concept.

Bob Hope, of course, is a Face, and it reminds you of despair. God knows why, it just does, and there it goes, down under Moods. Keep moving like this. Don't stop. You won't have to *use* all these words and ideas in the next part of this experiment, so if you have a little inkling to put something down, do it. You're not committed. Try to get a goodly number of items in each column, but some columns will have more than others: writing has a mind of its own. That's OK. It's temperamental that way. Keep writing. As all the great Gods of writing say, and say again, "Keep the pen moving."

OK. Let's try!

Your page might look like this:

MY IDEA FOR A NOVEL ABOUT THE INTERNATIONAL TRADE IN MONKEYS

Scenes	Questions	Moods	Concepts	Faces
A tropical nature preserve in Bali	What is Nature?	Curiosity	Theft	A gibbon
Rave in an abandoned winery in the ghetto	What is my path in life?	Boastfulness	People Alienated from Nature	Sean, the South African Journalist
Crowded apartment in Osaka full of birds in cages	Can tourism protect the environment?	Fear	International Financial Markets	The female DJ at the Rave
Tea Stall in the French Quarter in Hanoi	What can we do about social climbers?	Disorientation in a new land	Nature Preservation	Mark, the huge man playing sitar
African Game Park	Can we communicate with Animals?		Intimacy with "The Other"	Drunk Indonesian Sailor
Balinese Bungalow with a thatched roof	What are these people thinking?			An orangutan
				Taeko T, the painter in Bali
				Jared, the Trustafarian
				Local president of Wild Bird Society of Japan

Now what? Now is step two!

The thing to do is to choose just one item, one tidbit/kernel/chunk/radioactive nugget from any one of the columns and put a number beside it. The number "1." Choose the nugget that you think it would be interesting to start with, the one that intrigues *you*. And place a circled number beside it, on the left.

The next thing to do, the interesting thing, is to range your eyes all over that piece of paper—any column is OK—and choose *another* item to go next to the first. We are not going for "flow" here. In this instance, we think flow is *bad*. We're looking for disjuncture. What would be an interesting leap? What would be a non-opposite, dissimilar connection here? Not logical, not illogical, just interesting to you. That next kernel could be in the same column, but likely it isn't. Whatever. Just choose. Go with your gut. Put number "2" next to that. Keep going. Choose one link/ leap after the other and move forward. Go up to nine.

Now here's another interesting part: writing the piece. We're going to burn right through these "chunks," through these ideational tidbits, these place holders for larger inscribings, in a timed freewrite. Timed freewrites look like this:

- no turning back
- no scratching out
- no hesitation or staring into space
- no stopping at all (repeat the same word again and again if necessary)
- rush along furiously
- get it all out
- if anyone tries to stop you, shout "Get outa da way! I'm comin' through!" (this is called connecting with your Inner Banshee)

It's important to keep writing.

So: the writing of it. What you'll do is write one "chunk" for each number. A "chunk" might be a few sentences. It might be a paragraph. It might be only one sentence. Or a disconnected phrase. Or just a person's name. You write that chunk in any way or style that you want. And then move on to the next item, *with no transition or padding*. That's important. We've been taught to move smoothly, putt-putt-putting "the reader" along. (Who is that by the way? Some abstracted mannequin? Humans are variegated—we do so soon forget.) We've been taught transitions of logic, indoctrinated into a regular Ex-Lax ideology of slithering from one milquetoast concept to the next. No! The mind likes to move around haphazardly: let it jump. Also: keep your eyes on the clock. Twenty-five minutes. Or maybe you've got an egg timer. Or even better, one of those Wizard of Oz hourglasses. Fit in all nine chunkers in your twenty five mins, even if you have to stop midway in a bunch of them. Move ahead one leap at a time. Each item or piece stands alone, and it makes no apologies for itself. It doesn't need to be written any particular way. If something unexpected and disconnected comes up, put it down: "Welcome, Friend! Come right in!" Move forward.

It's nice, also, to be able to ring a bell for yourself at the beginning and the end. The mind responds to sound, and those bells were designed to take us to a deeper place. So why not use them? Tibetan bell, church bell, tinker bell, typewriter bell, why not?

OK. Now let's write. Set the timer. Ream through the nine chunks. Go like mad.

QUESTIONS FOR THE CURIOUS:

(For after you're finished.)

So there it is. You've finished one piece. If you're with a friend or friends,[1] you can read it aloud to them. Read it slowly. Don't explain it. Tell them you are not asking for their opinion of its "quality" or—heavens-to-Betsy—their *fixing*. If you're alone, you

---

[1] There are a lot of great ways to work with this stuff with other people and groups with a lot of added goodies of perception in Chapter 9.

can walk away from the page, get a cookie (or even milk *and* cookies), stretch, take a short footbath, listen to part of some song on a radio station you never listen to, and come back to the page.

You could, of course, skip the footbath and all that, and just read what you wrote right away, but sometimes it's a gift to read and listen to a piece with a different mindstate than the one that wrote it. It's hard enough to perceive your own work. Maybe when you were writing you were able to lose track of what you were doing? If so, great! If not, that's OK, the track-losing, not-knowing will come when you've graduated to even more Profound Levels. You could also just *not* read it at all, and move on to the next technique. Follow what you want to do.

If you do want to read the piece, watch your moods and perceptions as your eyes move down the page. How do those gaps you've created work? (The gaps between chunklets.) How is this different from some other way that you write? How does your mind respond and make meanings from the piece? Were the leaps between Outposts of Thought creative of new connections in your brainy-brain-brain?

One more thing: it's interesting to start to become aware of (sort of on the side) what emotions and thoughts are going through us as we do this freewriting business. What rises to the surface of awareness? What's freeing? What's annoying? Those Zen people call this the "second attention." How does your mind respond to this particular kind of experience?

But do be careful about Mr. Judge there: it may seem unusual to write this way. That's because it is. Whatever happened to you during the writing, there's no need for it to be the way you expected it to be. Let the mind have its way.

THE MIND OF IT:

In this piece, what we did is to *juxtapose* different parts against each other. The orangutans right up against the international financial markets. What's the connection? That's an interesting question. Really interesting. Let's not pre-decide an answer to it.

The mind is made of parts. Or at least that's one way to think about it. (The map is not the territory.) And these parts "Cankersores," "Xylophones," "Gila Monsters," "The Victrola Phonograph Company"—have been segregated from each other, kept apart, by the habitual patterning of our lives. Level-headed editors keep such things separate. There's a reason for all that, I know, but in some way, when we've adopted these isolation chambers of thinking as real and immutable, we've given up some of our freedom.

So what happens when they get put together? The way I have experienced it is that each word—which is really a chip, a piece, off that massive granite boulder of all human experience—connects to a series of memories, ideas, and emotions all over the brain (physically-located, electro-liquid network in the brain). And when we place pieces, chunks, rock-salt-to-crows-feet up next to each other, when we juxtapose and place in relation parts that aren't used to being with each other, synapses flash together, and stored up energy is released. It makes us laugh, or brings us to a deeper, more wise, or even more wacky place.

And that's why bringing a spirit of inquiry to what is happening can be so rich: We're open to seeing what happens and why.

TECHNIQUE THE SECOND

Oysters in the Mouth
(and Gravel)

What is writing made out of? Really.

It's made out of sounds. Word sounds. Syllable sounds. Letter sounds. One way of breaking into this is to use some handles. There are *liquid* letters, *l, m, n* and *r*: they do not stop. Lollapalooza. (Now why do people like that sound?) Lisp. Luscious. There are *aspirates,* they have in them hissy breath: *c, f, h, j, s,* or *x.* Throw a hex on those hicks. Fantastic. Fish. The coccyx. One also can speak of *mutes,* or two words I particularly like: *glottals* and *plosives.* Gag me with puck! A cack cack cack. Stopped breath. The words "glottal" and "plosive" themselves. Get back! Dapper. Torque. Duck!

Word sounds are physical; words come out of our bodies, and our bodies respond to words. They reverberate through our physical beings, coming up from gut to larynx, through glottis to vibratory tongue and gums, teeth, lips. And they travel then through the air and enter into the ear canal, cochlea, the spiral channel, and they vibrate the micro hairs, translating then into electrical impulses (at incredible speeds) ricocheting through the brain. And these electrical systems are linked—soldered by God— inextricably, with the living musculature of our full beings: lymphatic system, goose-bumped arm hairs, back of the neck, tendons in the grip. All of us responds to words. So why do we ignore it? We're told not to hear it, taught not to watch the physical resonance.

Paying attention to the propensities for odd words

A few sentences back, "soldered by God," I wrote. . . . don't know where that came from . . . wanted to break out of the overly scientific lingo-jargon place . . . started thinking about circuitry, electrical engineering, circuit boards, (those green plastic plates kids get in an electronics kit) . . . searching around the territory of the ideas for "connected" . . . and got the word *solder!*— that gray metal stuff, liquidy-looking . . . and then I thought, "Who did that soldering?" The back of my ear rhymed it with God. The oyster in the mouth!

And afterwards, there's the pleasure of the sound pattern in there, the freaky little "l" in the middle, throwing the "o" sound back, ever so slightly, into the throat. I can hear it in my mind.

So that's what we're going to play with next.

TRY IT!

This is really easy. We're using lists again. Write down words. Words that you like. In a list down the page.

Listen for sounds. Follow slick slipper. Use place names, words from many languages. Klickitat . . . Clackamas . . . Snoqualamie . . . Kalaloch. From the world of prescription medicines and disease, Glaxol, fibrocystic. The words don't have to be "nice;" pay no attention to what they "mean." Serbian Bisquick. People's names: Neruda. Darth Vader. Quakenbush. Even (and especially) words culled from sound: Blammo! Kablooey. Bent. Dunce. Gunk. Ilk. Include a short phrase or two if it comes to you. Boop boop a doop. Lazy around with certain sound slipperiness: larynx, lasagna, lascivious, laser. See how they sound. Feel them in your mind's mouth.

Nerve endings essential for hearing

Leave no stone unburned. Sports heroes. Technicalities of commodities trading on the Chicago pit. Underarm deodorants. Hindi film stars. Krill. Types of scar tissue in sub-atomic particles. (OK, made that one up. What does it matter?) Range far and wide. Gather sounds.

> Without conscious
> device we constantly
> reach into the vast
> word-hoards
> in the depths of the wild unconscious.
> —Gary Snyder

Take about ten minutes to make your list. Till you get a goodly batch. Wilderness of sound. OK, go.

Now we're going to put some of these babies together. As for meaning: well, we *could* deal with that. But why? Obsessively clinging to meaning is a kind of nervous tic. Neurotic almost. And it's a shackle on our freedom. Let's be done with it! We're looking for texture. Put these sounds together. Repeat them. Redundant. Redondo. Rudolfo. Rudimentary. Rutabaga. (Rutabaga, Rutabaga.) Make a "piece," whatever that means. Maybe make it dense on the page: six or eight words jammed together in a line, just to promote the schema in your mind for density, clotting, jamming things together. Add in a "the" or a "but" or an "I" or an "and." Use a particular dyad or triad that pulls at you, that pleases. Follow your interest, follow your instinct. Set the timer for ten minutes. And go.

QUESTIONS FOR THE CURIOUS:

Did ideas creep through? Did concepts form of their own accord? Inklings? Note how the mind is a pattern-making animal. If we don't shine a halogen searchlight on the poor squishy sensitive organ, see how its parts school like thousands of silvery fish. Perhaps there was only sound texture. That is good. Does your piece bump and slink? Are there places that feel aerated, chasmy? What ways did the density, the curdling of words and rhythm progress for you? Or was it open-y "o"s? Didja have fun?

THE MIND OF IT:

Words are made of sound, like I said. Even the remnant but un-vocalized sounds, secreted away in letters—"p" in "psyche" and "g" in "gnome"—we hear them. It's different, that sigh, that sci-ence, that site, that cyborg.

Now look again at what you just wrote, those packed words, thinking of those categorizationalizations I talked about, those liquids and plosives, and read the piece out loud. What do you hear that you didn't at first? If you can quiet your body, and enunciate the words, in a quiet room, you can feel where things resonate in the chest, rasp in the mouth, ungh! in the gut. Feel your physical human body which makes sounds. The body exists (though we're often told that it does not). Hear the timbre and pitch. If we focus on it—and here is an important piece of this work—if we direct our subtle attention to the sound, the very *sound* of words, this sensitivity infuses our life. It gets brought to the surface of our writing, and we hear it in everything. The lapping of the bay against the posts of the pier. The burbling of the samovar as it brews the spiced tea. Those anise-cardamom spice sounds smoke cigars in our mouths.

TECHNIQUE THE THIRD
Glimpses through Fog

You know when the fog parts and you see a little . . . piece . . . a part of something: maybe two people talking to each other on the street, one of them is incredibly tall, stooped, and bald. The fog closes up and you see something much farther away, bigger: a hillside. Then, to the left, in the middle distance, a Studebaker. You glance down at your own withered hands, back up and a great blue heron is there on a telephone wire, next to the Joe Camel billboard.

Glimpse
snatch
snippet
fragment
jolt
scene

Let's do it with words.

TRY IT!

Choose an incident. Or a time in your life. A five-year biochemistry experiment that got botched. You and your brother, trying, still trying to get along. Teaching organic gardening in Bulgaria. When you went to Louisiana for that family reunion so long ago. A superlative friend that you don't get to see anymore. Anything that has the faintest recognizability as a story will work for this one. Write down a phrase to hold the thought there at the top of that open page in front of you.

Now. We're used to telling things chronologically. And then . . . and then . . . and then. That's not a problem. But what if you had a reel-to-reel tape of this story, and had, just for example, Richard Nixon's secretary just accidentally erasing all over that tape? Didn't she have a footpedal or something, or that's what he said anyway, and it's useful for our trick here. Let's just say she had restless leg syndrome all over your narrative.

Or, think about it another way. Some censor was reading all your barracks mail, blacking out every "and," "which," and "that," and lots of here-and-there parts as well. The story is told, but as though in fragments, glimpsed through fog.

So in this piece of work, instead of *weaving* those glimpses together into some kind of clever narrative, we're going to leave them as they are—a series of impressionistic flashes, torn pieces from the newspaper of life.

Here's a hint from a piece I wrote on my first morning in Hanoi, a couple of years back.

> Horn honk, "I am here" sounds from the street below. Yellowy-smeared sunrise of crooked antennae, roof tiles, flower-pot balconies: all the little greeting cards of third-worldliness. Last night coming in by taxi, the air Stalinist-gray with soot, charcoal smells over the oxen fields and corn-planted bottomlands then into torn-up streets, sand piles, truck noises and winter-clothing people, industrious. Distressed patina of a revolutionary ambience hangs in my Hanoi thoughts: a chipped, fist-waving red-paint sign despite Sony TV in my hotel room. Four busy stone masons squat on the sidewalk carving gravestones; burdened women run by with pole-balanced baskets hanging from their shoulders; our waitress at dinner smiled big toothy embarrassed in the noodle restaurant. The soil from which Vietcong arose?

Now what if we were to get in there and add all kinds of explanatory connectors? If I were to have written: "When I was getting a ride into the city last night by taxi, I thought that the air was so gray, it reminded me of Stalinism, and there were charcoal smells and I saw out the windows oxen in the fields which were planted with corn, and then next I. . ."

Can you feel how much less the piece is by adding that information, those "of's" and "and's" and "or's" and "at's" and explanations of where what was when, and why. But by just listing fragments from memory, incantatorily, rhythmically, I could get myself, and perhaps a reader or two, to somewhere completely else.

The point, of course, is not to imitate this piece—imitation is contrary to liberation—it's to provide us permission to do less, to subtract. To piece bits of thread and gardenia and the Holocene epoch all together in a single bound.

O.K. Now let's get back your topic, to that phrase you wrote on your page to hold your place. Now roll your eyes back in your head and see just one image in your mind, and you can start with that. You can put down any impression that comes to you—sensation, memory, conjecture, hope—one after the other. Put them down without any transitions at all. It might be a quote, an image, a cry of despair, two sharp short views out the window—don't pause to figure out what goes best next. Better to put something broken and wrong and rude in there than to stop the pen. Not stopping is important for the mind to begin to let go.

And because you invite radical disjuncture—or anything—to come up, something surprising might. Go ahead and ring the bell and write for about 15 minutes, pen directly to paper, image, image, go!

QUESTIONS FOR THE CURIOUS:

What kind of journey did you go on? Did the mind make links where the words did not? One of the ways to work with this kind of material is to see what different ways it *could* be read. Try reading it now. Could multiple meanings be imputed? That would be good. Also what are the different textures of feeling you had when writing it, versus when you were reading it back?

THE MIND OF IT:

As you write words in the "glimpses and snatches" mode, you invite the mind to move in a way that it is used to doing, but perhaps unused to seeing in writing. The mind recognizes this way of moving, though, and finds it pleasurable. It relaxes and expands. The more you encourage it, the farther it goes. This is what we're going to be doing throughout this book: spurring the mind to go in directions it finds pleasurable, and new.

Also! Fragments and glimpses create spaces between things that are usually tightly caulked. In the spaces, the possible connections are implicit, or unknown. And it's in that gray area between implicit and unknown that—when conditions are right, and the moon is in the seventh house—the scimitar precision of the mind begins to blur, just slightly, and we enter into dreamlike states of not knowing, of possible guesses. And sometimes when the fissures between fragments yawn like a chasm in front of our minds, we become aware of the presence (always there but usually unnoticed) of all that we deeply, deeply do not know.

Not knowing is good. It cleanses the brain.

TECHNIQUE THE FOURTH
Shape-Shifting Writing

A newspaper story represents one way of seeing the world. The transcript of a dream gives us another. Each a different system of knowing; both of them true. A government study, and a myth of creation: one contains data, predictions, sureness about Truth. The other, magical deeds, Water, Land, and Sky. And sureness about Truth. Neither allows "I."

Genres of writing: each is a set of facets with an outlook on life. Journalism's "Five Ws" tell us exactly what to say. No wild conjectures, spell castings, or barked orders. Don't use the word "insalubrious." Or say "Georgie is a spastic dork!" Or "Stage Left:

Amanda walks toward center stage haloed in dry ice carrying a large beeswax candle, singing 'Nearer My God to Thee.'"

The words "gender" and "genre" start with "gen," the idea of a type. Boys can't carry purses, women don't fell trees. Can't do this, and don't ever do that. Abstract philosophy doesn't give dates or street addresses. It trucks in complexity, lofty word choice, and tells us how Being affects Knowing. It disallows teddy bears, rinky-dink gadgets, and words like "jerk off."

An analysis and a confession. A rant and a blurb. A love letter and cereal box text. A memo and a threat. Each has its options and its "Do not go there." Each of these widgets, these thingies called "genre," prompts specific characteristics and casts taboos upon others.

TRY IT!

For this game, again, you'll want to have a Topic, but the game works better with a concept, feeling, or question instead of a specific event. Here're some examples, by people I know: "Israel-Palestine." "Gluttony." "International Finance As It Relates to Prostitution." "My Mother Has Alzheimer's." "I Wish I Could Live in a Houseboat."

A storyteller (and a darned good one), told me this once: "I write down six or seven stories I know on a card a few hours before I perform. When I walk up on stage, and look out at the audience, I glance down at that card and sense where I'm at. I choose the one or two stories that most fit my mood. I'll tell them for real that way."

That's going to work well for us, too. So reach into your memory hoard—or notice what you feel just right now—and choose a topic that means something, that you can connect to. Write that phrase at the top of your page. In the next thirty minutes or so we're gonna write and stay with this theme, and along the way, at junctures, you will shift suddenly to another world of writing, without missing a beat. An excellent way to hit up the subconscious.

The first time we do this, this shifting of lenses, I'm going to give you seven different genres to write through. They're listed below . . . but wait! Knowing in advance will subtract from your surprise, and your surprise is the phenomenon that can be relied upon to help you stumble upon the subconscious.

Here's how it works: you start on your topic and write any way you want for a couple of minutes. No genre yet. You just get rolling on your topic: "Peter does not want a child." "If only I hadn't been so frightened." Then once you're rolling look down below at the list—not yet!—and then shift into that style of writing, but stay on the same topic. Go for the specified number of minutes, and jump right to the next genre on the list. No transition or padding, *gziipp* right ahead. But stay with your theme. If a particular genre seems hard for you or hard for this topic, No Matter! Just make it up, or do a parody, or lard it with clichés and cheesy catch phrases. You'll be surprised how they sound on the other side of finishing this piece. Just keep the pen roaring. Just say "Yes" to what comes.

The getting rolling part

THEN Personal letter (3 minutes)

THEN To-do list (3 minutes)

THEN Dialog with stage directions (5 minutes)

THEN Fever dream (2 minutes)

THEN Confessional ("Bless me, Father, for I have sinned.") (4 minutes)

THEN Mega-hype advertising (3 minutes)

THEN Furious rant (3 minutes)

THEN Prayer (3 minutes)

QUESTIONS FOR THE CURIOUS:

Discover anything? Laugh with surprise? After you've read it back, how did you perceive the lack of transitions? We underestimate the mind's pattern-making, pattern-perceiving abilities. The empty space between the genres gets filled with the rushing winds of imagination. How does that fever dream talk to that confessional?

Were some of them "harder" than others? Moods shift in this circus parade of rising and lowering curtains of the so-called "self." Certain genres shimmy out easier than others, but this changes with topic and time.

THE MIND OF IT:

To write an obituary, a confession, a memo, a rant: each one is a filter on the fullness of life. Yet—and this is the cool part— since they each were earmarked with a purpose when Joe made them up, years ago, they represent relationships between people, moods, and situations that exist in real life. They are codified echoes (obituary, rant) of ways we relate, and each of them then reverberates in an area of the brain. As one theorist put it, genres are "fossilized social interactions": ways of relating between people, ossified patterns that have hardened into sets of "Do" and "Do not." A genre can be a liberation or a genre can be a cage. It's a cage when you are about to express your love for the children of the African village in your policy report, and you know that you cannot. It's a cage when you have to flay the dead horse of econometric analysis in your thesis when you want to write about power inequalities in the places where people work, or when you have to be "character driven" when the arc of the story is about place as it groans under the tyranny of time. But a genre is a freedom when you can shift to dream text or to pathetic sniveling in the middle of your freewrite. All kinds of things are allowed that before were not.

One of the purposes of writing at all is trying to figure out what really happens in this life. That gets harder, though, when we've pre-decided that "lurid travel brochure," "resume," and "ransom note" have been disowned and disparaged and kept out of the realm of our journals, our stories, and our poems. But they live in our brains. They are ways of relating between humans, and communicating one corner of truth. Thus, when we let them consort with each other, one after the next, the allowable territory—the proportion of life that is touched, probed, and known—expands and encompasses more of what's true. Then what we are writing becomes less of a lie.

Now! Mess with them yourself:

I've got *lots* of these herbal infusions called "genre" for you, wildcrafted over my years. And I've tried them all out in my classes: taxi-tested tough. So now you can puzzle-piece together your own sideshow from the Genre Smorgasbord. That's on the next page. Put them together for yourself or your friends. Choose them at random or plan out a sequence. They are yours to command, these patterns in the brain.

A GENRE SMORGASBORD

academic paper
sad reminiscence
statistical abstract
advice column
letter of complaint
"to do" list
obituary
fairy tale
abstract philosophical discourse
newspaper article (who, what, when, where, why, etc)

set of instructions
company's annual report
confessional
explorer's log
narration of crime
factual description
luscious description
chronological sequence
recipe
plaque on historic building
demure coquettish prattle

surrealist play

compare and contrast essay

songs of praise

shopping list

feminist literary criticism

junk mail

historical biography

tone poem

definition

slave narrative

summary of the main points

compassionate letter of sympathy

channeling of other-worldly being

pathetic sniveling

legal deposition

lurid description of exotic
    travel destination

thesis, antithesis, synthesis

resumé

holiday post card

polemic

trance induction

over-the-top New Age hype

love letter

ecstatic nature writing

trashy romance

hero's quest

clinical description

sutra

inter-office memo

hate speech

cause and effect essay

limerick

disclaimer of liability

sarcastic hipster's snide remarks

letter to the editor

tear-jerker

code of discipline

seduction

dream text

logical proof (if A, then B)

market survey

psychology journal article

paranoiac rant

righteous manifesto

soft porn

dispassionate analysis

science fiction

a personal letter

insecure, incoherent
    journal entry

chanting invocation of
    the gods

scripted dialog with
    stage directions

schmaltzy musical comedy

barked orders

country-western ballad

prayer

"he said, she said"

suicide letter

"Just the facts ma'am, the
    cold hard facts"

prissy hissy fit

market forecast

guided visualization

political diatribe

slapstick farce

museum catalog

homage/ode

a jingle

celebratory remarks at a
    black tie dinner

joke told in a bar

self justification monologue

field guide to birds,
    flowers, nature

mega-hype advertising

product warning

greeting card

TECHNIQUE THE FIFTH

Writing What You Don't Know You Know

Here's what "they" say about writing (again and again): First you gotta get your ideas straight. Nail that concept down in your head. Then translate those notions into clear precise words. Write those words down through fingers and pen. Know what you're knowing and see it on the page.

Well, it *sounds* logical. And "logical" it is. But man cannot live on bread alone. (And dry dusty bread at that!) Thank God there's another thing. I've done this, so I can tell you that it's possible and true: Your fingers can write a thought you did not think.

Check *that* out. You get in a state of Utter Permission, and the words come out fast. One word after another, strict kaleido-chaos. No joke. Ass-over-teakettle, lickety split. You don't know what you've written till you read the words back. Departed, abstracted, the intention-mind gone. It sure *looks* like your handwriting, but "Did I really write that?!"

Here's some of that butter brickle cackle:

> . . . soupy sales dig down deep ding dong doll it's
> scary it's hoary it's genuine it's preamble to the suffix suf-
> focate the quinine waves lifting birds crated and surely
> missing from peach fuzz corn bread corn pone penchant
> for gone hunting I can't tuned to the one sore loser gated
> community ich sprechen none of your business beach
> head bird brain If I was a tillerman I'd weave a how d'ya
> do mine eyes have seen the samsonite the island again
> gross hock spit. . . .

We'll save the *why* you would want to write this way for a detailed discussion afterwards (hint: *actual freedom*), but for the time being, let's get you to a place where you can do it. Some hints and clues: Automatic writing. Surrealists. Paris. The '20s. Freud and the unconscious. Artists in cahoots with explorers of mind.[2]

TRY IT!

So the basic instruction is this: Write down words. *Any* words. And quickly. Don't stop. I know you didn't stop before, but now *really* don't stop. There is *no topic* for this writing. Write the first word that comes in. If you get stuck, write the same word again and again—byzantine byzantine byzantine byzantine quack! Keep going until something cracks. Let your eyes roll back in your head. No sentences, no syntax, no meaning, and for God's sake no goal. Just go.

You could start now . . . but what if "it" isn't happening? What if you keep meaning to write what you write? Here are couple of tricks (use them if you wish):

Trick one:

Poetic ruptures.[3] We've got to get those industrious little elves of meaning in there to throw up their hands. Get out a book of poems. Just yank it off the shelf. It doesn't matter who it is, or why. Now, when you sit down for your ten minutes, what you'll do is every so often (and at unpredictable times) open to a random page (that Goddess of Chance!) and read out a phrase. Four to six words, no less and no more.

Copy these words down, verbatim entirety, in the middle of your screed, and charge on from there. Do it again in a minute.

[2] You want to know the learny-reference booky stuff? OK. In 1920 the surrealists Soupault and Breton absconded with the term "Automatic Writing" from the spirit medium types. They took old Sigmundo Freud's theorized entity, "the unconscious mind," (whoa!) and came up with a method where that squishy entity was invited to speak directly to the page, bypassing the ego's logical filters and the super-ego's prissiness. But let's not just think about it. Let's do it.

[3] Good thanks to the Maestro Leslie Kirk Campbell of Ripe Fruit School of Creative Writing for the idea on this! Thanks Leslie!

Do it again in three. Keep interrupting, and baffling that brain. After jilting the intentional mind one time and two times, and three times and four, the logic craniometers will just hang up their hats, leave in a huff—and that's when you break free. Just keep saying to yourself, "Write *any* word." Write "the." Write "ichthyosaur." Write "bilge pump." Jostle into the crowd of sound. Whatever it be. Keep writing, not stopping, till something else can emerge.

Trick two:

Or! Sit by the radio, tuned to AM, and periodically, (or a-periodically) just punch that "power on" button. *Three seconds only*. And then punch it back off. Copy down the word frags they dumped in your brain, and keep at it in your trance.

OK. Now you got it. Set off into the poorly-lit night. Crack the champagne against the hull and cut the mooring ropes, and byzantine quack.

THE MIND OF IT (WHAT IS THE PURPOSE OF THIS?):

What *is* the Purpose of this?

There's *no purpose* in doing this. None at all. Or that's the trick, the way it will work. If you're trying to do this to strengthen your style or leaven your mind . . . guess what? It works. But if you think, "Gimme gimme gimme," and "I want I want I want," you will annoy the deity in whose favor you wish to remain.

Yes, this has helped me in my Work, and in my life its very self. And that's great now, it is. But do most people go skiing to take videos of themselves skiing and show them to others? No! They ski for the experience of skiing, for going downhill. That's the Rumpelstiltskin of this. Do it in order to do it, and see what else can happen on your page.

You might get your brain more limber. You might find a phrase that seismographs your entire readership. You can use it in your screenplay. You might discover some information or data or wisdom. All of this has happened to me and to other perfectly well-adjusted gerbils. But it works best—really, really—to do it just to do it, and find where your mind wants to ski.

AMASS YOUR PLENTY
(OR, "I WANT / DO NOT WANT TO WRITE ABOUT")

So far we've played in two realms: One is to sit down with no topic, no goal in view and open the gerbilly mind, and find out what we don't know. That's the automatic writing bit we just tried out. And the oysters. And the other is to take a thematic gambol with an idea-topic in mind and then write through one of our faceted games to find new ways to see it. Such so-called "topics" could be anything: my dog, class struggles in Silicon Valley, the incurability of arthritis, changing perceptions about the sex industry, and cetera.

We've got a lot more still to mess with in both of these realms, but for the latter, the thematics, right now we're gonna amass a hoard. Abundance feels good. This listing of topics will give us some more Spirograph pinpoints around which to cog our gears.

So here's what we'll do:

A new page, a line down the center, all the way down. (Who knows? You could even scratch this list on one of the blank pages at the back of this book, since we're going to pull from it again and again.)

At the top of the left side, write "I Want to Write About" and on the right side top, "I Do Not Want To Write About." We'll do a listing of topics all the way down.

This is a flashbulb-instant portrait of what you feel like and want right now. As you fast list, you put down anything that glimmers with even a "maybe might." You're not promising that you will and must write about this; it's just an avaricious stockpiling of whims.

Put lighter fluid on your wants,
and let them fuel the night.

What about the right side? Sometimes we define what we want through what we don't. You might want to Not Write About money worries 'cause you're sick of cycling back around to that. Sometimes, saying what you don't want identifies the corrosive material that's eating away at your true pleasure for writing. "No, I don't want to go there. Not again."

Or maybe "Not Write About" whittles an even finer edge on what you Do. "I want to write about being bullied in school," but "I don't want to write about the individual bullies, or what they wanted."

Also, one side of the list may provoke another. "I don't want to write about violent scary men" on one side tells me that "I do want to write about soil, water, trees, wildfires, birds, and Buddhist meditation."

You'll notice an interplay as you write—especially if you invite it— between one list and another. Topics you don't want to write about may migrate tomorrow. An item may jump ship from one side to another. "I don't want to write biotoxins! I thought I did but I don't." Or the other way around. "I've been saying I don't want to write about her death, but you know what? I think I finally do."

Another suggestion: do this rapidly. Too fast to try to "figure out" why. Just get down a list, as long as you can, even if you have to suddenly write "frijoles" in one column and you have literally no feelings either way about beans. Just keep writing and listing for ten minutes or more. How many can you get, how big a list?

Plenty is good. Muchness be praised! Blockedness cannot withstand the tide. Having many things you want to write about by your side is a good woodstove of comfort should any times of want blow your way from the frightened North. Be interested in the world, and scribble it down. Even if you never look at this list, having it there, even having experienced the copious grapes on the vine, heavy and sweet, tells your mind that there is no want. Keep this list by you, ready to let it grow, time and again.

It's also good catapult fodder for any of our experiments to come. (And don't forget to look backwards through the book, trying these different techniques in different ways and at different times.)

And let us also, before we start this list, say a thank you to Not. The "Do Not Want" honors an important inner part of you, the sourpuss-bah-humbug-sick-and-tired-spent-and-revolted-disgusted-and-through-with-all-that inner self of you. Long live Ebenezer Scrooge! Now let's try it out.

Subliminal Realms: Dropping into the Deep Subconscious

Everyone has experienced trance, altered states of mind. You wake up at 4:30 a.m. and you remember a lover of a decade or more ago. Vividly. That's trance. Daydream: you're at your desk and suddenly fifteen minutes have gone while you've accomplished nothing. That's trance. Or a fever dream. All different. (And *that's* interesting.)

What are altered states? No one knows, no one understands. We know they exist, and we know that they have a feeling texture different than the "it's-2 p.m.-at-the-office" mind, the "gotta-run-those-errands-and-get-back-here-in-a-hurry" mind. Trance happens in the mind and writing happens in the mind.[1] They interact. They *could* interact more. And more. Part of this work is to say to the mind, Sure, you've got a lot of figuring capacity. Yep, you've got lots of functional departments. Yes, if we let you, you can create the entire Department of Health and Human Services, Department of Parking and Traffic, and The Department of Rules and Regulations for Poetry. We're proud of you. Good figuring mind. We're glad you can do those things. Invent us some product-interface software.

---

[1] Perhaps neither of them originates in the mind, but for what's happening with our writing here, it doesn't matter.

But also. Remember that, being human, you can also slither out of sight of the staple remover sitting on the desk there and sneak off to find the bubbling mudflats oozing with burnt molasses.

And the more we whisper "the mudflats" to the mind, the more it listens! The mind is really a good dog! Tell it that it can perceive the difference between cold mist off the ocean and cold mist off the dry ice factory, and in due course, it can. Tell the mind that it can abrogate the treaty it has made with two plus two, and it can. Indeed it already has.

The second part of this is: Watch these trance states, feel them, and they change, deepen. And if we change the mind, somehow, as we're writing, the writing changes . . . of its own accord.

TECHNIQUE THE SIXTH
A Shifting Book of Images: The Tarot

Cards. We love to play! They fall out of the box and separate from each other. Let's put them together—in different ways.

Pictures. We relate to them as they activate our minds. Chance, the Goddess, she intervenes. We welcome that.

The ancient past. A territory of the subconscious (which we forget!), operating below the stratum, working on us all the time.

Somewhere back before we were here, a system of mysteries was enunciated, put into images, by those foreign people of that time. All the images together, as a system, is a machine that can work on us, that worked on them, that work on us *because* they worked on them.

Collected on pieces of portable knowledge, on cards, in the unbound book known as the Tarot, these images, the shifting network of them, point at the root nodes of human experience. They are a map of experience in life and of consciousness in its weird and unbridled guises. They've been fine-tuned for a very, very long time. They are a dictionary, a reference book of self: The Lovers, The High Priestess, The Hermit, The Devil, The Fool.

Because the pages (cards) are free to associate with each other in multiple juxtapositions, they are a non-linear text. They have many powers: first we have the associative power of images—images catapulted into the distant future, that is, to us now, by those who came before. And then. And then! We have the ability of the cards to reassert continually different sequences, connect in different ways. Having both of these potencies gives a particular access into the inarticulable, druidic realms of our as-yet-unknown interior. You can drop into trance.

a foggy, imprecise interior

But maybe you are one of those people who have No Idea what the Six of Cups means. Congratulations! This will be easier for you than for those folkses who know all kinds of hocus-pocus about Celtic Crosses and Significators and cetera. Those who do know all that stuff have the handicap of being forced by their own minds to think that The Tower means X and does not mean Y. If you do know those correspondences, there is still hope for you; do not despair. You just need to let go of the Meaning and let the colors and shapes and images free of their pre-ordained connection.

TRY IT!

Got a deck of tarot cards? Ones that you like? (OK, go out and get another if the impulse takes you.) What kind is best? Well, the decks that have imagery for every single card, not just four swords on a desolate blank field, work much the best.

For this trick, we will let chance be in charge. You have no topic, no question, no superstition, just openness to experience, and images in your hands.

The first thing is to sit like a kid there on the floor, and turn the cards face down, and mess them up. Go ahead. Keep messing. Let 'em get good and mixed. Till you feel that they're mixed.[2]

Now reach in and choose, one after the other, eight cards from the face-down pile. You choose the ones you are drawn to just from their backs. When you've got eight, you turn over these cards, hold them in your hands, look at their faces, and watch yourself respond. Feel as you look. The less you "know" about the cards, about their referential meaning, the better.

There's two of them that you don't like. Put them back. Now look at the ones left. They are in your hands. As you look, you see colors, faces, directions that the faces look, moods, light and dark. Let the pictures move you, as they were designed to do.

Now put them in a sequence. Any sequence they want. As one goes before another, they turn into a "piece." The piece has movement in it. It moves your mind to a different location.

Now run through the cards, beginning to end. Run through that sequence again and once more. Now you are noticing the spaces *in between* the cards, the flow of the cards as they shift from one place to another.

Feel also the energetics shift from one image to the next. You want to page through the cards many, many times. More than you'd think. You want to page through from beginning to end enough times that your mind stops focussing on the individual cards but focuses on the entire story, the entire shift from the start to the finish.

Now you are writing a rapid timed freewrite. Seventeen minutes or so. Although you *could* write *about* the cards—"I got the hanged man and it means that I have to wait"—but how Ho Hum is that? Writing "about" is so restrictive, don't you feel? "This equals and means that." Why not instead write *from* the cards, let them sway your feelings, let them suggest and hint, let the colors dilate your mood. You may be glancing at them occa-

[2] Fun with friends!

sionally in front of you. Or you can write just from the feeling state created by the cards, not looking at them at all after you start, writing from the eddies set in motion by the stream of the cards when you were running through them.

Ready, set, go.

QUESTIONS FOR THE CURIOUS:

Before you decide what happened for you and what did not, I recommend reading your piece back. Often things happened that you didn't notice when you were writing on through.[3] Try walking away, making a kind of tea you usually don't have, opening a window you usually don't open, looking out that window at an angle you usually don't look, and then coming back, and take your writing to another room, the back porch, and read. Can you see energies or concepts or movements or patterns you didn't see when writing? If so, be pleased. To get to a state in which phenomena are occurring that you are not aware of when writing is one of our goals. 'Cause that means that something other than the conscious, in-control mind had got hold of the reins.

THE MIND OF IT (ME THINKINGS):

The Tarot is not just about divination or predicting the future. Images were collected by the ancients, and they were encoded in a kind of game ("Will I marry a tall handsome stranger?") in order that their wisdom would be propelled, compelled into the future.

The Tarot images are symbols, pieces, and parts of fundamental human experience or universal laws, fundamental energetics that exist in this world—The Death Card, The Judgement Card, The Magician Card, The Tower. Each card, with respect to the others, is migratory and ambulatory. Their movement sug-

---

[3] Actually this is what it's all about: writing what you didn't notice you wrote.

gests to our mind that each of *its* parts can also do the same. They hint to us that these pieces of ourselves can interact and play with each other. They cue our minds to treat parts of life as malleable and migratory.

Also, Tarot decks themselves are changing. People make new versions with new pictures and new wordings; every year more. These are new kinds of knowing through image, color, and line. As new decks emerge and change, still they retain tracery from so very anciently long ago. Just like your words, as they shift you through time. Sing their praises. Continual mystery! Inexhaustible. Good.

TECHNIQUE THE SEVENTH

Falling into Natural Beings/ The Lure of the Sensuous[4]

> Perception ... at its most intimate level ...
> is a coupling between the perceiving body
> and that which it perceives.
>
> —David Abram

What shape experience? I mean actual experience of the World. Not just to *describe* the chipped paint and spider webs behind the cardboard boxes in the garage, and the way they appear to our visual brain-cortex and language-making system; not just to describe that, but for the psyche to *enter into* it. We want to get close to it with face and mind, yes, but also with the intention to let the objects we perceive in this life, whatever they are—a cat's eyes, chipped paint, sea urchin, chipotle salsa—take

---

[4] Let me give great protestations and loud bellowings of Yow! to David Abram, who (through the medium of writing!) gave us the book titled *The Spell of the Sensuous* and gave me much more experience of the World— vivid—and started me figuring about how to do what he spoke of, by use of writing.

us over, to have them completely grab the controls of our sensibility, amplify and pivot our consciousness.

Usually, we're cluttered and clogged by *thoughts*. Concepts. We can't see the tree. I'm not speaking of the *idea* of "the natural world," but the pug-nose, real-deal, fur-scruff, bone-duff nature. How does *this* stone feel different?

Pine two-by-fours stacked on a shelf
    above your head at the lumber yard
Caramel corn and salt-water taffy
Dry vermouth and tenor sax
Fresh blacktop stretched like a tight rubber band
between endlessly reiterating Saguaro cacti

What if we abandoned all our learned hoity-toity that we have about sea urchins? All the facts and figures, theories of nutrient biotics? What if you set aside all your knowledge and prior theoreticalizing, your logic analyses and your backlogged store of facts about this phenomenon (the urchin) that you have in front of you and just saw it? What direction does it take you? You have a vague sense of it, but that's not enough: Follow it. Define it, but don't let the defining stop you. Perceive and become porous. And (important!) tell yourself you can. Barn door wide open. Try it for more than 25 seconds. Stay with it, that salsa, its taste. Close your eyes, right there in the Mexican restaurant while your coworkers are yammering and plunge into the texture on your tongue. Now let it have the controls. You are its abject slave. Yes, you still see it through your mood, as it changes, and you still see it through the fuzz in your eyes and the crick in your neck, but even so, you only see it through who you are at the moment, and not through a bunch of conceptualizations.

What am I talking about? Let me say:

Pomegranate.[5]

---

[5] (eating a pomegranate)

Just reading the word there, I'll guess and bet you've remembered the succulent amniotic sac of red lusciousness surrounding each annoyingly astringent seed (mealy inside), or the dripping of said nectar down an inconvenient part of chin, perhaps even turning the corner and heading down in the direction of neck. Am I saying something you haven't experienced? Didn't some version of this replay across the screen of mind when your brain decoded the four syllable word, Poh-Meh-Gra-Nit, above? So when you ate the pomegranate, you couldn't read the newspaper at the same time, right? You gave yourself over to it because the magnanimous and yet bossy nature of the fruit itself demanded it. This is why I call the pomegranate a "being." Let us treat it so.

With more attention to the act of eating, with an intention to taste the luscious and to avoid the pucker, to not spill the wombful of seeds on the floor as you ripped the leathery skin open, you in some way attuned yourself to its "presence."

> attuning ourselves to the presence
> of this being

So here's the gig: you can do this attuning more and more in your days on Earth. You can do it with everything. Everything. Even the chew marked Number 2 pencil there. Even with the seat-back tray table in front of you. And we can do it via writing, not just by "using more descriptive language" and "more precise observation of the thing itself," but by vibrating our molecules in sync with it while we write, in sync with the pomegranate, in sync with the glowing yellow eyes of your cat.

And, the exciting thing: we can call up that closer, more scintillating connection by actually *using* the uncooperative nature of written language— its inability to perfectly fiber-optic-cable from one brain to another, its inability to exactly transfer the world of our experience onto a page of paper—as an advantage. (I've done this.)

Language resists, and that helps us, goads us to going further, to trying harder, to persisting. We want to push against the less-than-pliable nature of words, to find a different docking port between world and self. Pushing against gives us contact with all the sensate hullabaloo that physical reality has for us to feel.

TRY IT!

Choose a being. Perhaps a wilted flower. Something handy, something from nature: flint, clump of leaf mold, something unglamorous, a pigeon feather, or perhaps a snakeskin, or a chunk of broken granite. Or if you're feeling contrary, something not "natural": a battery cable, Uncle Feldspar's rusted switchblade knife. Choose it because you like it, or because it pulls at you. Put it in front of you, and take note of your space. Your interior space.

Part one: depict, just depict

Now start with describing this thing for seven minutes or so. Try not to do it in an obvious way, or—God save us—a clinical way. Just watch the being, and keep the pen moving and stay with exact looking. Precise precise precise. Focus on the small. Even smaller. Do not take refuge in reason, nor in cause and effect, nor numbers and figures, nor graduated cylinders and Ph strips. And also observe—lightly, with the corner of your mind—how you shift internally as you write. Finish. Now move to part the next.

Part two: inter-being

David Abram says, "Humans are tuned for relationship." It's true. A thousand centuries, we've been honed and sharpened and whittled into the perfect instruments to sense what is around us, what we encounter. So even though we've lost most of those skills of acute perceiving that our forest hunter ancestors had, that doesn't mean that our bodies are not still tuned and sharp for sensing things far beyond what we believe we can. It's all in there, in you. Being a human, with your billions of brain cells, you have all the equipment necessary to feel this other being, gel with it, chill with it, meld into it.

> To define another being as an inert or passive object
> is to deny its ability to actively engage us
> and to provoke our senses ...
> —David Abram

Allow the heretical belief that this stone has meaning, and you will discover that it does. Are you going to join all those xenophobes and self-superior Enlightenment types who say that Native Peoples do not read messages in clouds, that they are "just imagining"?

Our intention is to feel all the aspects of how this being is present before us. It's the difference between the number of times we've heard the phrase "see the world in a grain of sand," and the number of times we've actually tried to do it. How far back into that grain of sand can we go? How far back can we follow water? The mountain out of which it seeped? The river valley it carved 3,000 centuries ago? The shatterings of light it throws against the wall in the morning?

So look at it again and let this being in—the abalone shell, the burnt-out lightbulb. Notice—and see how your perception shifts if you really invite the waves of it into you. We are not just looking from ourselves and describing the Other like we were before. We are letting the actual waves of its light enter through the gate of pupil-retina to cortex of brain. Molecules of light and sound and smell are pouring off of it and are now entering the delicate mechanisms of your sense organs. Thus it becomes part of our real actual mind as we gaze at it. How completely can you let yourself say, "OK, senses, infuse me with the sound, with color and shape, abscond with my mind?"

As I contemplate the blue of the sky . . .
I abandon myself to it and plunge into this mystery.
It "thinks itself within me" . . .
my consciousness is saturated with this limitless blue . . .
—Maurice Merleau-Ponty

Now start writing for ten minutes or so. Same being, but now you let it saturate you as you form letters on page. You fall into its trance. Keep writing words, any words that appear to you, like you did in Technique the Fifth, Writing What You Don't Know You Know. You are beyond description now. You are writing your relationship to it, and you are writing the inside of yourself. The writing keeps your attention to the being in front of you: put word after word. Don't try to figure, just keep scratching at it, keep scratching words on the surface of page. That the being resists a perfected embodiment in words is part of this too. Keep going into it. Maybe a strange word. Maybe just a sound. Maybe a disconnected phrase. Keep writing. And the more you give yourself to it, the more you surrender to its way of vibrating (and I really do mean to use that word), the more it will infect and impact you. The more you invite, the more you get pulled. After ten minutes of writing whatever comes out of the end of your pen, you stop, ready for the next.

Part three: the "do not know"

Perceiving is always unfinished. Open-ended. You cannot know this being totally. It is not only that we as modern people have had our plant knowledge wiped out, that we can only wonder, "What does it mean when the seagull cries just like that?" when our forebears used to know. That knowing we have lost, true. Grievous. Yet it is not only that. There's a fundamental relation we have—almost always ignored—to our own *inability* to know. Our not-knowing can provoke in us different responses. One response can be a guessing: the imaginative mind. It's the provocation of curiosity. That same provocation wriggles around behind all the starch-shirted, glaringly white pages of research in *The New England Journal of We Know It and You Don't.*

But all our curiosities, all our guessings, the hunches and hypotheses, the provisional attempts—though exciting—are avoiding the more profound emptiness of "I just do not know." The vast howling emptiness: the mystery, in its literal sense. That's the gateway through which we may enter. Can you touch the truth that you cannot know dog? You may call him "dog." You may even name him "Spot." You may live with him for a decade, watch him. But fundamentally, you do not know.

Now, to write. Again return to that being, the granite or salsa or snakeskin or battery cable. Look and do not know. Write your not knowing. Write from the unknown. Ten minutes again.

Don't foreclose on that not knowing with a vow to find out; neither turn away and say, "Well, it's just one of those things: I cannot know.'" These are, in some sense, closings. Just sit with what you don't—and maybe cannot—know. Move the pen on the page responding to the unknowing and watch how it accumulates within you over time. Keep moving the pen. And watching that mind.

QUESTIONS FOR PERCEPTION:

Look up from the page. Change your seat, go to a different place. Fresh air yourself. Now read that first few lines from Part One of this freewrite. Look back at the being. Note how your relation to it has changed by means of the writing. Read over (with appreciation and curiosity—not evaluation, of course) the three freewrites. Notice, if you can, how they changed in the writing of them. What are the results of your experiments? How about the last part, how did the holding of "I do not know"— without turning away, nor researching, nor guessing—but just not knowing, how did that change you? How did it change the way you wrote?

THE MIND OF IT:

The texture of your experience may be admixed with the time of day, your energy state, how full or empty your tummy is, but this texture will also be part of the being you are relating to. Gazing at the nicked switch blade will be different than gazing at the crystals of salt. The things of this world do participate in the fabric of our consciousness, inflect who we are each moment. We may ignore this inflection, but if we give attention to it—and we can use writing to do this—the reciprocity and inter-relatedness blossom and grow.

TECHNIQUE THE EIGHTH
The Gateway of Place Memory

"Long, long ago . . ."

Now *why* does that work on us? Why do we go away? "Far, far away . . ." We drop down into our own minds: the imagination and memory transport our consciousness, and *place* is the gateway, a long ago place.

TRY IT!

Choose somewhere you visited once in your life for less than ten days. Somewhere that reverberates for you. You know that place because its views and scenes sneak up on you at times of yearning. Maybe a city in Eastern Europe. You left wishing you didn't have to go, "If only I had longer to stay here, but I can't because . . . " A small green-grass town in upstate New York that you sped through on the way to someplace else.

Place is our gateway: Santa Catalina Island in the sea . . . the Bitterroot Mountains . . . a river valley in the Shenandoah . . . Venice

. . . . Less than ten days. You keep returning back to that place in those unplanned moments. Choose one place, and write down the name of that place to hold on to at the top of a blank page.

> Sooner or later we come upon a city
> that is the image of the inner city.
> —Anaïs Nin

Now put your pen down for a minute or two and find yourself a relaxed spot in a position that feels good to you. Unplug the phone. The mind is more kind to requests for relaxation when the body feels safe and good. You will do your own self-relaxation, and it works better with eyes closed. You may read this first and then go through it again in your memory. Or you can have a friend, a good trusted friend, read this to you.

Feet on the ground, lean back, let the muscles ease. (The eyes don't mind closing.) Scan the body; say this slowly to yourself—feet, legs, abdomen, chest, arms, throat, face, scalp, whole. Let it be looser. Breathe a deep breath. Breathe another. Please, a third. Keep letting, giving yourself permission to allow.

Now you can revisit that special place inside of your mind. Go there. Embark. That one place. What do you see? First the colors and the quality of light. Shapes. Seeing those things now. What do you see? Look around, walk. Are there people speaking? Animal or bird sounds? Fall deeper into this place. Your memory was a memory made by your senses: they are available to you. Tell your mind that you can *be* there. Enter deeper into the paths or streets. Smells. Wind? Heat, or cold. Feel the air on your skin. What other feelings? Stomachache? Disorientation? Drunk? Farther down into the textures in the muscles. The sense of touch: what did you feel?

You have the picture, you have the images and feel, and gently, you come back out and return to the room in which you are sitting. Try to come directly to the page as soon as your eyes open. And now you start to write. Write glimpses. One after another. Keep your mind deep in this place, keep your eyes filled with its sights. Let yourself rove over them again and again. You could, of course, just write *about* this place, but the trick of this one is to really *drop in* to it. To mull it in your mind like spiced cider. Fall into the trance of place. And all that requires is egging the mind on. "I can drop deeper. I want to. I want to fall into this place. I *love* being in my memories."

Follow the metaphors that arise to you. Why did you keep returning to that carnival mask shop? The way that light played on the glade in the mid-late afternoon, with the leaves slightly shifting. Is desire pulling you? Let it. Your impulse urges you toward a turn down that street. Watch how you are wanting as you write, but do not stop writing. . . . *edge of a building turning a corner . . . foolish thought you had at that time . . . smell of bread . . .* What you didn't realize until just now: an inkling.

After you've written for fifteen minutes, bring your mind back to the room. Look around. Stretch. You don't have to read what was put down.

PART TWO: THE IMAGINATION IN MEMORY

We're going to be doing a part two here, but first let's clear the brain, splash the face, change something. Or two. Sit in a different chair.

What we will do soon is to re-enter the place you've been. It has come alive for you, and it changed and shifted with the words you wrote. The words have added to your experience of it, not just "recorded" it: the words change the memory.

Before we return to this place, though, we're doing a deeper trance this time. You'll want the room to be very quiet. No interruptions at all. And again you'll either have a gentle friend read the induction, or you'll read it slowly to yourself with eyes half closed, remember its sequence and cycle through it again in your mind. What you are going to do for yourself is something called "self hypnosis." It's no big deal. You simply are going to do a slow, full-body relaxation to allow your mind more freedom to roam. Forget all the clichés you've heard about hypnosis. You simply let the brain relax the body, one part at a time. You've probably done this before in some form or another. We'll get the body totally comfortable, methodically making sure all these parts are relaxed, and then we'll re-enter the place we've just gone to, but now we enter in *imagination*: we let the mind do what it wants to there, not just what the memory says actually happened.

Sooooo . . . you get into a comfortable place. Ahhhh. More and more comfortable: adjust anything you need to. And in a second, you'll close your eyes. When you do, first tell the body that it *is* OK to relax. The less the muscles are gripping your poor bones and organs, the less attention the brain will have to give to them, the more space it'll have for falling into the place memory, for letting you be resilient, lithe in your imagination.

Let's start.

Let the kind attention of your caring mind come slowly up through the body, starting with the feet. Feel your feet, the soles, the between the toes. Soothed. Soupy. Easier still. Ankle bones . . . the calf soft, loose, easy, releasing . . . knees, tendons loosening. *Nice!* Feels nice . . . thigh muscles, skin. Pelvis, bones in there, actually relaxing, internal organs . . . don't *want* to be clutched like that. Let the poor things be. Allow. OK. It really *is* OK. Follow this good soothing feeling up . . . belly. Belly, low back. Release. Good. Side of the abdomen, little muscles along the side of the spine. In between each rib. The *lungs.* Ahhhhhh. Why not be sweet? You feel pleased. Muscles of the chest. Loosening. Soothed. Shoulders. Arms, flowing downward, like a lava lamp of warm goodfeelingness, oozing over. The arm hairs even floppier. Wrists! Fingers! (Poor fingers. Gripping the pen.) Let them loose. Fingers of each hand. Palm. Easy. Easy. Thumbs relaxed. Now perceive the whole arm, and the whole torso, and all of the legs, feel that they are soft.

Now move up into the neck, throat, little tendons that were holding in there dissolving into sweetness. Now the jaw. Lips. All those muscles and musclelets that had been taking up iotas of attention, let them loose. Nose . . . eyelids . . . muscles around the eyes . . . back of the neck . . . scalp, top, front, back, and sides. Now the inside of the head too.

The whole body relaxed . . . the whole thing. Notice that. Scan the body and feel that it is indeed good and nice.

Now picture yourself at the top of a staircase—a well-lit and safe staircase—and at the bottom there's a door. The staircase brings you deeper into your trance. In your imagination, you will walk down each stair, counting from ten down to one; and on each stair you will tell yourself you can feel more relaxed and more full and complete. Each stair step down, enjoying the feel of being deeper in trance. Step ten down to one. Each one a pause, counting in your mind.

On the last stair step, you put your hand on the door, and you open the door. On the other side is the place that you were writing of before, and you can enter it once more. You are now in that place again. But now you can go beyond what your memory tells you, and you *imagine* what happens; you go where you want to go, do what you want to do, meet whom you want to meet. Respond to your yearning: if you desire to do it, please do.

Give yourself some minutes to wander . . . and, at a time that feels right to you . . . you envision in your mind, without opening your eyes, your journal and your pen back up at the top of the stairs. Now you move back to the door and come back up the stairs, one up to ten, count them to yourself, and easingly, gently, come back to the room. Move right away to the page and *start moving the pen*. Don't let any space come between to ponder, or gap out. Just tell the pen to move on the page and record what you saw, writing glimpses and pieces: don't take the pen off the flow of the mind. Ten minutes, you write and you write.

QUESTIONS FOR THE CURIOUS:

Did you notice any difference between first trance and second? Did taking the process of induction more fully the second time change the texture of your experience, the texture of your language? Also, did you notice how in this technique we are writing a kind of reportage afterwards of what was experienced in trance? This is different from writing at the same time we are in process, as in some of the techniques we've played with before. Was the quality of experience different as well? (You liked it more, you liked it less?) Another interesting thing to investigate is how the first burst of writing changed the way you experienced the second. Writing itself is a kind of trance, isn't it? How does one trance infiltrate the other? A good question too: Were there places in the imagination that you chose to avoid? Were there times when you took the risk and plunged forward despite?

THE MIND OF IT:

We're working with three powers here. One is the way words come differently out of a body at ease: The mind moves in a different kind of way. Language gets produced from a deeper well. A second phenomenon is the way we have access to memory, and that is through location. I read once that to improve your recall of dreams, and to improve the vividness of your dreams, you should—during waking hours—practice being aware of spatial relationships: noticing the shape and contents of rooms, the way three-dimensional objects fill up their space. This is because the subconscious inhabits space as well; it lives in the three dimensions. Memory is also spatial. By remembering the details of a room, a streetscape, a view down into the canyon, the memory itself experiences a place to be. The senses created the memory, and they have left their remnants in a tracery of synapses all over the brain. We fire those up again when we remember those places and call them to mind.

The third force of nature called to our aid in this gateway to the subconscious is the imagination itself. Of course a relaxed body imagines differently than one that is tense. And when we invite the imaginatory powers into the realm of memory, to change what has been recorded as true, we're inaugurating a very fundamental liberation in the structure of the mind. You'll be surprised at the connections that blossom when you do.

Shatter/ Scramble: Finding the Power of Fragmented Meaning

Everyone's afraid of being called incoherent. We are supposed to connect all the parts. That's all good, but when the writing muscle gets bound by habit, by repetitive motion, the machine-mind creeps in. You put the cups in the cabinet, the forks in the drawer, you take the exact same route home, and you write a grammatical sentence. Suddenly, you've got habits, tendencies, and tics. We make certain connections and abandon others, or forget they're available.

Soon we feel: "Prison!" We try to—but can't—think our way out of this problem. Our joints have become stiff. Loops and loops and loops, over and over. They become the obstacle, and you lose the quirk.

Think about it this way: your mind is prone to move logically or associatively from one thing to the next. Electrical impulses make grammatical sentences, over and over, and the circuitry becomes reinforced, grooved in a rut.

How to get you back to where you want to be? Simpler than you think: just unhook the brain wires and reconnect them anew.

Put the old pathways in new orders (a lot), and see what transformer arcs leap across the untraversed spaces. And the cool thing is, we can do it with a simple cut and paste, with a no-intention mind. We just need to stop trying to *accomplish* something (even for a minute); we need to let go of the authoritarian directives of our minds to always know *what* we're doing, and *why* we're doing it, and to be in control of how it will turn out in advance. This is what's causing the problem! Let go of the Sense Chaperone, and the Purpose Hall Monitor, and just be open to what randomness and chance might produce.

Voices heard, things seen, "the way things are done":
they sculpt pathways in the brain.
Patterns repeat themselves,
and the pathways are grooved.
We become steeped in our context, used to our patterns,
and so it's hard to be new.

TECHNIQUE THE NINTH

Shuffle the Nuggets, Re-sequence the Mind

One thing leads to another. A headline leads to an explanation, which leads to a quote. A long, long time ago leads to a galaxy far, far away. The coffee leads to the bagel; showing up at work leads to the paycheck, which leads to the rent. The same thing happens tomorrow. Patterns repeat themselves and we know what to expect. The synaptic electrons flow down one neuro-rivulet in the brain and not down the other. Soon they are eroding the bank and a gully turns into a channel, and it's hard to think new. Newspapers, emails, weather reports, phone conversations, exposés, self-help books: all have their sequences, each grooves a track that gets harder to budge as our days are patterned by the texts we imbibe. We are like those people announcing departing flights by the gates, saying the same thing over and over, again and again. "Passengers travelling with small children . . ." "We'd like to welcome our business class hamsters . . ." "Have your boarding passes ready for the agent . . ." They're probably getting a repetitive stress injury of the brain, even as we speak. But it's not just them. We're all in it together. Language is the stuff of consciousness, a very major part, and we run in its groove.

We talk like Mom and Dad. We write like what we read. We gurgle forth movie clichés, and we don't even mean to. Our attention moves from a sound association, to a glint of light, to a memory of some dumb piece of office politics from the '80s to an out-of-date slogan . . . .

What to do?

TRY IT!

You'll want to start this one with something already written. But anything will do. It could be a page from your teenage diary. It could be a letter you found in a box in the attic, written by your great uncle to someone named Sue. It could be your short story. You can use the newspaper. Some terrible thing. I used the newspaper several days after the abominations at Abu Ghraib first hit the press. (I guess I don't need to say this—with the reality of this world—but your writing doesn't all need to be "nice." This world is full of rust holes and epidemics, cancer wards and corrosive hazmats. If words can represent it, then it's material for use. We're trying to recombobulate the mind.)

**The words have something
still in them for you.**

If you want to start with a new piece of writing, you can just scrawl for five minutes on some event or other and write, "and then ___ , and then ___ , and then ___." But get yerself some words, words in a row.

Now go through and look for outcroppings of interest. Underline a short phrase/part of a sentence—three or six words, nothing too long, but more than one word.[1] Underline another. Get at least seven. Or nine. Odd numbers are good. And when you choose phrases, follow your instinct, follow what you are interested in, follow what seems to be calling to you, or troubling you, or intriguing for whatever reason that you may not know.

Follow traces curious curlings weird puffs of smoke

When I do this, I'm usually choosing *everything* of interest, and I end up underlining more than seven. But then when I go back through again, I know which seven I'll really want to mess with. Take a few minutes. Go quickly. Don't think too much.

kernels that may yet expand

Copy each of these phrases onto a separate small scrap of paper. Index cards work swell. (Liberate the poor index card, tarred and feathered by research papers and fluorescent light. Let it back into the world of play with its cousins the Tarot cards, the Jack of Diamonds and Queen of Hearts!) Or just use the napkins there at the diner.

Now take these little shardlets, these culled nuggets, and shuffle them around. Mix it up! Invite the holy god of Random into the core of your piece. Let chance be your birthright, your ticket. This works best if you shuffle them blind. With your pen and journal at the ready, lay them out in a row.

Look now at the flow of the chunks, and get ready to write. You will expand the piece back out again, stretch it back out to size. You can put in anything at all, but keep those same words, and keep them in that new order. And the freedom part is this: it can become a *completely* different piece. Maybe the same topic, maybe another. Maybe you turn it into a tone poem, or the story of some made-up person. Maybe you don't *know* what it is—a

---

[1] . . . unless of course you're Breaking the Rules . . .

paean to uncertainty. The secret to transforming the piece (and your mind) is to allow anything to come in. In the spaces between, you can insert jelly doughnuts or NASCAR dads or nitrogen phosphate: anything. The only thing is to keep these very same words in the order that they're in. Spread the shards out through the new piece in any way you like, some close together, others farther apart. How good to not be shackled by "sense." A deeper sense can happen than you can control with your brain. Set the timer to twenty minutes, move all the way through, and see what you find.

QUESTIONS FOR THE CURIOUS:

Did anything happen here? (It doesn't have to be cataclysmic—though it might be—we're just lookin' for somethin'.) What grew in the cracks? Connections unlooked-for, omens of the gods? Was the new piece like the old one in tenor and pace? Or was it just the faintest tracery, aurora borealis, in the domed back of the sky?

THE MIND OF IT:

In re-arranging a sequence—whether you use random arrangement or some intuitive intention—words connect and combine. Juxtaposed objects spark the mind to create. ("Why is that there?") Usually we write by connecting pieces of text by logic, by chronology, or by "that made me think of this," which creates in the reader the feeling of "flow." But shuffling the nuggets sparks a "Huh?" and a pause, and a wanting to know. There's a field of speculation, of guesses and clues. And since words connect to synapses, new leaps are fomented, new patterns are grooved. The rearrangement of phrases creates a new brain.

Let's move to the next!

MISCHIEF THE TENTH

Counting Splice!

Let's not think about this one too much. Let's just try it. A jump to how to . . .

TRY IT!

Take a piece of writing that already exists. We're gonna mix it up. If you want, try this with something written by someone else, from the newspaper, or a novel you read in seventh grade (or a book report you wrote in seventh grade!). Using someone else's piece can relieve you of the tremendous gravitational force of What I Have to Say. You get good at releasing, and then you can go back later and try it with your own piece. Or you can dive right in using something you wrote last year, or yesterday. Perhaps pick a piece that feels stuck for you. Perhaps an unfinished dissertation, a vexing essay, a stream of words that somehow got roadblocked. Take about half a page of it and pick up a pen.

OK, ready? Start with the first word, and start counting words. One two three four five six *seven*, and underline that seventh word. Now count again, . . . five-six-*seven*, underline that word. Now do it again. Every seventh word, underline. Doesn't matter whether the word is a meat word or a potato word, or just an "or," or an "a." Keep going. Get yourself to twenty-five words or so underlined.

Now copy these words—and these words only—on a fresh blank page.

words disconnected from their sacred moorings

Next: read them out loud and sense the "connect" or "imply" that glances sideways from behind the words. Now a short freewrite, five minutes or so. Keep those original words in that order, but fill in the cracks with something . . . in any new way. Some words of the original close together, others farther apart. Same topic or no. Experiment with both ways: be open. Don't matter. Fan the flames. Follow any thrust that suggests itself. Get through the end, five minutes, fast.

QUESTIONS FOR THE CURIOUS:

Did you see yourself trying to make it all sensible again? Or did the side-angle twisting curve ball of illogic free you to mischief it up? Did new meanings gopher-hole out of the ground for you? What did you find?

THE MIND OF IT:

There's a power, a mystery, of associative, fragmented meaning. We beseech it for its gifts. Words in their old order, their logical-rational order there on the page, have a power, an inertia just by being there. The way the piece was before this number-count splice created its own gravitational force field. But, also, by just being there, the new sentence, "we Odd the getting it can't milk," creates permission. And the mind likes permission. It's been held down for far too long. "Hey!" (the mind says) "If *that's* OK, think what *else* we could do." Unusuality can sneakily, mischievously pop up, jack-in-the-box up, in the middle of the formal, black-tie snoot-fest, and romp its shaggy wet-dog hair around and let people laugh, loosen up the belly (the mind's belly), and (Lo!) other confabulations happen. Thus, "We calculate the harebrained Odd fricassee which was the way of getting ourselves to the top of the mountain. It harbingered a sausage factory which can't ever be milk."

Don't worry that it doesn't come out useful for your final exam. Life is full of time, especially for such jewels of loosening the mind. The child does not regret time spent in play. And, guess what, sometimes it *does* come out useful for the final exam. You can get the just the right word (entire *books* can pivot around having just the right word). You might get a new concept, or a new feeling about the piece. Or you might just have galoshes full of fun, because, as I have emphasized previously, a harbingered sausage factory can't ever be milk.

you go into the illogic
and come out with poetry
(or something)

STRATAGEM THE ELEVENTH
Scissors and Tape

"Cut and paste" used to *mean* something before the word processor. But even back then, the idea was to go for "flow." Flow means Maalox. Means goes down easy and smooth. While no one here at Writing Open the Mind is advocating cruelty to the reader, the invocation to "flow" is vague and tends to homogenize, tends to limit, and that's not the goal. We want to promote the unexpected, the odd. Which means (in this case), we want to re-chunk. And let it not be said that we worship only at the Church of Odd. Sometimes the process of creating a piece is jagged and jumpy, but it doesn't mean that the finished piece of writing can't run through the soft fingers like fine white sand.

But we *are* the enemies of flat. And while you could try to spice things with the front of the mind—you know, toss in a cuss word, or a fist fight, or a used condom or something—if we really want to storm the Bastille, we need more radical change, to rolf the sequence and discombobulate the set.

TRY IT!

Copy a piece of your work on a copy machine. Or if the piece is on the 'puter, print it up twice. Put the original away and well out of sight. Sit at a big clear table. Nothing but you, the pages, and the scissors and tape.

And cut. Cut into chunks. Too micro and you get confetti, too few pieces and you don't break the trance.[2] Four sentences here. A single phrase there. A whole paragraph and a half over there. Enough to have plenty, not so many as to confuse.

Spread them out on the wide open space . . . and mix up the parts.

There are two ways to try in terms of intention: Random Disjoint or Intuitively Connect. Try both, but try one first. The former punts the decisions to the Great Gods of Chance; the latter lets the will of the whiff connect pieces in an oblique but vaguely-guessed way. Try one or the other, based on your unquestionable interest, pleasure, and whim. If it's total scramblography, just mess it all up blindly with your toe. If it's Intuitively Connect, look for an intriguing fit, but not for a flow. Either way, you want something unguessed of and new. Unprocessed. Tape it together, and you're ready to start.

What've you got now?

Now re-write the piece. You might fill in the cracks with corn flakes and tinsel. Or you might make smooth garrulous transitions flowing in like a dashing gentleman in a pencil-thin moustache and a black cape. You might do a new freewrite, a ten minute burst, based on a single juncture, a rough fault line, the rubbing of two sticks. Or you might start blank and charge through from start to end, a brand new piece, a brand new day: thirty five minutes straight. (Yes, write out the same words again, it'll do you good, you love those words.) What you do with it depends on how you react to the new thing you've made. What do you see now that you did not see before?

SKATING THE SPECTRUM BETWEEN RANDOM CHANCE, RATIONAL PLANNING, AND INTUITIVE INTENTION

> The surrealists emphasized the role of chance.
> Starting from the experience that a society organized
> on the basis of a means-ends rationality
> increasingly restricts the individual's scope,
> the Surrealists attempted to discover elements
> of the unpredictable in everyday life.
>
> —Madan Sarup

There is a spectrum. The spectrum stretches from the most rigid of order to the most Bozo of random. One end of the spectrum that you can use for your writing self is rational planning. This is the thesis statement. It is the abstract followed by the statement of the problem, followed by the methods, followed by the results, followed by the analysis and conclusion. The order end of the spectrum is the cause and effect, the compare and contrast, the chronology through time. These are ways to order your piece.

Then there is smithereens. Mix it. Break it up. Shatter the order. The palliative effect of smithereens. Smithereens can be good for you, although, depending on your mood, a little bit uncomfortable. The mind that wants to stay comfortable is the mind that is resisting.

Smithereens can feel rude to you, smithereens can feel like your important idea got lost. Smithereens can feel like something organic and whole has gone through the shredder. "I was just getting warmed up," says your mind. "But I liked that order! It pleases me." But smithereens makes you let it go.

Smithereens are random chance. Random. Chance. The value of randomness is that freed from the habitual patterns, something other comes up. There will be a new order, perhaps. Is there such a thing as patternlessness in writing? And even if there were, would people make patterns anyway with their minds? Maybe we can't know, but the thing is that smithereens surprises you.

Smithereens is not always the best, though. Dreams and redwood forests have their unity. Why put them through the shredder? Use smithereens with discretion.

Somewhere in the middle of the spectrum is intuitive intention. It's the pin-the-tail-on-the-donkey while slightly peeking through rose-colored sunglasses out of the corner of the eye. Intuitive intention is the "I don't know why, but I chose it." The baby moose in the dream.

This spectrum is yours; you are free to float anywhere along it that you want to. Experiment with stretching your limits. See what happens. See how you respond.

QUESTIONS FOR THE CURIOUS (INQUISITIVE!):

What's different about the recobbled piece? Did the logocentric try to resist? Didja get new ideas? Or new words? If you were to explain to someone close to you how it changed, what would you say?

THE MIND OF IT:

The human mind moves from one thing to the next. One thought provokes another. That's how we write: the pen records the words provoked, which stimulate and impel the next words to come forth. Thinking is links, a sequence of chunks. That's why the organization of your piece is the movement of the mind. In everyday life we think in a box. One thing leads to the next. The very same next. From synapse to synapse, electric impulses jump, linking one idea to another, again and again.

To break out of the loop,[2] we shuffle the chunks. It is the rewiring of sequence that disrupts the Known, challenges "order," and opens the can of worms.

What happens when illogical shuffling and scrambling connect those previously segregated chunks? The revision of structure is an alchemy of perception. We are breaking the tyranny of What We Already Know. New structure: new gaps. In the gaps, we are guessing, trying to relate. Guesses are linkages—they give us new pathways, and thus a new mind.

A new form often must be created
in order to express a radically new idea—
and knowing a form with which an idea can be articulated
improves the likelihood of thinking that idea.

—Richard Coe, "An Apology for Form"

[2] de looptie looptie looptie looptie

Sway: Triggering New Mindstates with Scent, Light, and Sound

Incense smoke. Incense smoke is perhaps the best metaphor for what happens in Sway. You catch a whiff. You don't always notice it, but nonetheless, you do catch it. There are different kinds of incenses in this world. There is that heavy, sticky, almost lurid Indian temple incense, cloying and erotic (in the spiritual sense). There is that refined Chinese temple incense, lifting you to the Heaven of the Ten Thousand Buddhas. There is that Roman Catholic incense pouring out of the censer as the robed priest walks down the aisles. Also true is the sage smudge of the Lakota sweat lodge. The smell incites and persuades you—each one *differently*. Here, in Sway, we will pull upon various elixirs, not only aromatic, but sensory, physical, and locational, and we will allow (nay, invite!) each to dilate our minds and emotions in their particular way, and then let that swayed place in us disperse words (through osmosis into air) onto the page and into the world.

Indeed! There are hundreds (thousands?) of distinct varieties of feeling and energy states. We shuffle through them all day, all the time. These internal states shift with the angle of sunlight, with responses to music, with the memory kicking up all kinds of internal voices, with states of health, and with objects in the world we see, which we desire or reject. The trick is to let that feeling state speak with as little interference from the conceptual or planning mind as possible. This is why we keep the pen moving and continually exhort ourselves to stay open, so that we can let words emit from that transmogrifying state.

What happens to the brain when it is victimized by the scent of baked bread or of cut grass on a warm summer afternoon? These aromas don't just make us feel good, they effect a certain *kind* of reaction, biochemical and supernatural, simultaneously. The caw of a crow fills the sky and fills your head. Everything in there shifts. And you write from that shift.

The guiding idea here in Sway is to shift the mind to a new state and then sketch the surface of your experience and perceptions as they crosseth the screen of the great movie theater of consciousness.

ENTRANCEMENT THE TWELFTH

Aroma Shiftings

Agreeable smells, Ahhh, there are so many. A nosegay. Mint in the sun. Crushed basil. Why do we swoon to them? They float through the air. Smell of ocean on the breeze, pine sap, dust in the sun, vaporizing molecules scattered from eucalyptus leaves, gardenia: they were meant to seduce. And we wouldn't (and couldn't) smell them unless they were "supposed" to do something to us. Why else would we have those receptors in our brain and our nose? I ask this of you.

The jasmine and the rose flowers of this world fill the molecules of liquid air that swirl like bath water around each bloom with their invisible outpourings. Picture cream in coffee—you know that swirling—waftings in the viscous liquid of sky.

An animal sniffs at pennyroyal, cedar bark, cardamom, to check the resonant brain receptors that tell it if the plant is nutriment or poison. How does it know? The whole body responds with desire or aversion, swoon or disgust. How does the animal distinguish sustenance from toxin? How does the bunny sniff the clover and know it is not hemlock?

The brain has its centers that are activated. Far, far back in the ten thousand generations of great, great grand-parenthood, we knew by scent the Yes from the No. We've been around plants that long. We've co-evolved with the complex chemistries of frankincense and myrrh. And just as we cannot hear the high pitch of the dog whistle because we do not need to, there are a hundred thousand scents we cannot sniff because we just don't have the equipment there in the schnoz, or the hardware behind it. So the fragrances we do smell, it seems, are perceptible for a reason.

Affect Lobes Triggered by Our Ancient Kinship with the Plant Kingdom

Willing and waiting, our synaptic receptors are there, thousands upon thousands, each one a finely-tuned petri dish all prepared and ready: one for spiced cider, another for the skank of sex, another for toasted sesame oil, another for dill on buttered popcorn, another for pine sap on the morning mountain air. Lo! A whole Library-of-Congress-sized laboratory of millions of petri dishes, each one ready to catch the spore of a particular scent of the World, incubate it in the echoing corridors of your vast consciousness, and grow it out from the dish like a vermicelli of sprouts seeking light. The nodes and receptors of the brain are ready for the appearance of whiff.

TRY IT!

Let's play with this. First choose the topic. You could pull from your hoard, your accumulating list of "I want to write about . . ."

(Growing up on the prairie? The friend you lost in high school? Why you sing?) Whatever it is, write the topic at the top of the page.

Now you may choose a harem of scents. But don't choose the scents *for* the topic. That's pre-determining. That's over-determining.

You can get your scents with incense, from herbs, fresh or dried; you can choose flowers and fragrant leaves from a walk around your neighborhood. The smell of dried and molting leaves is an excellent musty one. Or farm scents if you are in the country! Tuft of hay, leather halter strap from the horsey tack, chicken feed, corn. Or you can just take a cup of hot water and drip a couple of plinks of essential oil into it.

The process will look something like this: "I want to write about how certain kinds of men are really difficult for me to be around." And you go out into the World (which might just be your kitchen) and collect five fragrant things, different from each other, to sway you in your state. In your case, you might get pumpkin spice, a grapefruit, Earl Grey tea, essential oil of lilac, and an ashtray of cigarette butts. (Remember everything doesn't have to be nicey-nice and all New Age and pastel lighting and harp and synthesizer music and lavender pillows. Be real, like the world that made you!)

And now you will arrange the scents in an order, a sequence of non-opposite, potentially intriguing juxtapositions. You want to put them in their arrangement next to you now, handy so you don't have to think 'bout 'em when you light into your topic.

So when you are ready (and open!), start the pen moving and with your non-dominant hand—keep writing, no stopping, with the other—pull the scent-dispersing (blessed) item close up to the sensing organ, the delicate and sensitive nostril, and *smell*. Let the smell drench you. Inhale again and lurk into the corners of the smell (don't stop writing!). Let the pungency sway you, rattle your teacups. See if you can simultaneously keep writing *on topic* while the spooky part of your mind, the corner-snooping, curi-ous-mysterious side of your consciousness roots around with its snout in the crevices of the scent. Stay a little longer with the scent than you think you can, and then, no segue, move right into the next scent and keep going. Write from the mind that recog-nizes this scent: what does it have to say about this thematic that you are writing about? Feel its overtones and nuances, but do not write *about* this scent, just let it inscribe certain icicle patterns and desert-mirage shimmerings about you, and then let that state have its way with the words. Next scent, and next, and next. Keep moving. Don't ask too many questions about the petri dishes or word choice. Let the words appear, and you have no idea why.

It's not about why

THE MIND OF IT (OR WHAT I'VE NOTICED):

Something mysterious going on here. Whiff is powerful. Ancient mammal that you are, gene code that stretches back con-tinuous unbroken string for a hundred thousand centuries: the scent gives us information, the scent gives us feeling, the scent links us to the vaporous nature of the breathing Earth. All our ancestors, all our relatives here ("all our relations," as the Lakota people say)—the fish in the primordial ocean, the alligator, the wildebeest—all navigated what was important with the mem-branes of schnoz. Impulses got fired off in their body-mind sys-tem. (The sweet intoxication!)

In us, when the pungent lobes and locations of the brain fire off their electrons, they are wired in (crossways) to the vast store-house of language—also resident in the brain—that is waiting in reserve. The words cat-on-a-hot-tin-roof out of the brain and onto the page, like a pine-pitch igniting, the synaptic converter.

MANEUVER THIRTEEN

Through the Subtle Moodshift of Place

A location instigates a particular frame of mind. Office building lobbies spread their certain kind of miasma of mind space, and Third World marketplaces quicken another. Musty old parlors this, and throbbing dance floor basements that. The human animal replies to place. Architects study this in school. There are a hundred thousand shapes of places to be: a shaded ravine, a ship's gargantuan hull, crouching in a clutch of seaside grass. The amoeba of consciousness re-forms in response to the shapes that it pervades. And consciousness, as we've seen, affects what we write.

TRY IT!

Snag a theme. Maybe one from your list. Write it at the top of the page. Ready with pen and you take yourself somewhere distinct. You'll be doing two writes, one in one place, and then next in another. You don't have to get all elegiac about your choice of location. Start with the garbage room of the apartment building and move to the lonely degraded bus stop across the street for the other. Or choose places in your house: the attic and the basement; or the stairwell and the garden; or sitting right on the threshold of the front door and then huddled up in the back of the closet.

You may choose places outside and natural: under a low-slung tree—all surrounded—for the first, and then out to the very middle of a huge grassy field for the other. Or dispense with the natural: the vast empty parking lot of an abandoned mall and your local botanical garden's tropical plants room. Decide on your two places, each distinct from the other.

Now, again, the trick is to avoid "about." The evil "about." We want to be swayed, influenced, filled, smoked, snookered by this place we are in. But the topic is still the topic. That's why we chose it, not to just get bossed around by the place. Other normal regular people can write *about* place. That doesn't bother us: let them. We are letting the hypnotic of place throw its ghost nets over our promiscuous and willing consciousness.

> Memories and our old pathways are woven like ghost nets
> invisibly filling the landscape of our days.
> —Gary Snyder

So the freewrite. This will be the way: locate your body—with all its sensory organizmos—in Location One. Think the topic. Feel the place. Let and invite the location to color and dilate your mind in its particular direction. Place *always* does this anyway, but how different if we tuned our thousand tiny antennae to it? Your eyes have peripheral vision: they sense things on the edges. Be alert to the edges. The pores are alive to energy.

Now start writing, not stopping, keeping the pen moving at the crest of the mind. Ten minutes exact. Stay on the theme—your Spirit Guide, your dissertation, your vacation in Minneapolis, your coworker—whatever it is. And while you're writing, let the tendrils of your sensate self drink in the energetics of the place. Stop at Ten. Now—don't think or pause or nothin'—git yourself right up and move to Location Two. Feel the shift. All the sensors open. Tune the antennae. All ten thousand antennae. Now set the timer again, let the location con you, and write on the topic. Let the circus go on in the background. Be snookered and duped. Stay on topic. See what happens.

QUESTIONS FOR THE CURIOUS:

Does the world affect you? Does the world *effect* you? Did you get a different "feel" from your two locations? Did you feel yourself closed and open? Comfy and cradled and then windy and exposed? Could you sense the connections between your world, the Inner, and your world, the Outer? How did that connection change the words that you used?

THE MIND OF IT:

We are in the world. Definitely. Our bodies have for so many millennia been tuned to the scintillations of the planet. The physical ecology of the world sways our mindstate. It's always happening. Our thoughts, memories, and imaginations are a wilderness area. This wilderness area meets the boiler room, it meets the smoky Scottish pub, it eddies in the undertows of the muffler shop, the Latino bakery, the I.C.U.

Our bodies are wild.
The involuntary quick turn of the head at a shout,
the vertigo at looking off a precipice,
the heart-in-the-throat in a moment of danger . . .
the quiet moments relaxing staring reflecting—
all universal responses of this mammal body.
—Gary Snyder

Like a magnetic field, the energy of rooms and ravines inter-penetrates our porous membranes. Why don't you want to live in a dingy basement apartment? (Unless of course you're a Goth. But then, in that case, why is it that you do?) Cathedrals, mosques, Japanese tea houses, and light airy lofts: we choose these places to be in so we can nourish an innate part of us that needs to reach beyond the boundary of self.

The haunted house, the negatively-charged ions after a rain-storm: we can agree the energy of things and places exists.[1] You've got your own way to explain it to your finicky mind so that it can accept this. Call it by whatever mystical or scientistical term that allows you to stay with me on this.

But we aren't directly, vividly conscious of said energy most of the time. The interesting thing is that when we say, "Yes, let's have it, let's pull it toward us"—when we invite the elixir of place into willing, waiting, and aware perception—we become more *of*

[1] Perhaps words also linger in the atmosphere—as potential—to take shape again, in the next open-minding freewrite. The words shape us, take charge. I've seen it happen.

the world, and more excited by it. The twittering and hopping of little birds sends solenoid frissons through our biological system. The mosque soothes my soul. And if I keep the pen moving, it affects the shape of sound on the page. How good and joyous. Give Jah all the thanks and praises.

Let's move to the next.

QUACK NUMBER FOURTEEN
Dilated by Sound

Crow caws make you feel one way. Goose honks, another. Mysterious cries high in the rainforest canopy yet another. Black Sabbath. Cool Jazz. Women laughing. The swami saying "Ommmmmmm." A novelist I heard of puts on a certain kind of music when writing each particular character: she enters the authentic mindspace for that character's soul.

Neurologists are out there CAT-scanning skulls and coloring computer models of the brain in neon-glowing colors have put forth the proposition that certain centers in the cortex light up and fire their jets when the ears listen to sound. And as far as my sketchy, dilettante self knows about these things, our language centers are cross-wired with those that listen to sound.

TRY IT!

Got topic? Raid from the "do and don't" list. Or don't: Dial in your radio transmitter to what you want to write about right now. Or! Steal some topic from somebody else. Borrow it. Look up to your shelf of books just this moment: "Managing Your Money." Presto! Or the totally Bad and Wrong political event you read about in the newspaper this morning. Or something big and broad: My Love Life; The State of the World. Or tiny and long ago: Jethro Tull and Its Role in My Adolescent Imagination. Or cheesy and funny: Sonny and Cher. Or portentous and sideways: Rotting Leaves and Memory.

Now set yourself up. Maybe you've got a sound system? That's one way to do it. Choose two kinds of music. Or better yet three, or five. Make them different from each other. Put them in a certain sequence before you start so you don't have to think about logistics when you're writing.

Some hints: Give yourself a mix. Try for neither sameness nor opposites. Make one after the other different, but not too obvious. *Not*: "OK, this one's 'sad,' and this one's 'happy,' and this one's 'slow' and this one 'frenzied.'" Go more oblique, less obvious.

Also, are you someone who gets distracted by people speaking when you're trying to write in cafes? How about doing only instrumental music, or something in a language you don't understand?

Another way to do this is to try using sounds that are not "music." Get yourself a haunted house LP from the used record store. Or sounds of animals: whale and dolphin songs.

If you live in New York, you could go from subway station to subway station, laying your consciousness open at the feet of each different musician in those echoey halls. The thing about it is to have at least two different textures close to each other.

So now, having chosen a topic, set yourself up with title on page and get ready to shift auditory guideposts. Give, say, three to four minutes for each sound segment and write in the way that we know from before: glimpses, listings, the automatic response, little clusters of impulses. Tune your antennae to the subtle shiftings that happen in you with each soundscape. Drink in the vibe. Invite your various centers to open themselves to the vacillations of sound.

QUESTIONS FOR PERCEPTION:

So, when you're finished, go away for a second. Astringent the mind with something utterly else: lay a hot towel soaked in steamy water gently upon the face; or vacuum the carpet for exactly 120 seconds, and no longer. Clear the skull. And now come back and look at the piece. What kind of word sounds prevail in the text on the page? Shimmy-shammy sounds or clattery, clunkity, bang-bang-pow? Are certain sections bossier than others? Is a certain style abject and another virile?

THE MIND OF IT:

Those neurologist-Merlins might measure it with all their fancy imaging software, but the potency of the mind in response to sound comes from ancientness and the vast stretches of time.

> The world is as sharp as the edge of a knife . . .
> the sharper the knife
> the cleaner the line of the carving.
> We can appreciate the elegance of the forces
> that shape life and the world,
> that have shaped every line of our bodies—
> teeth and nails,
> nipples and eyebrows.
> —Gary Snyder

We keep the sacred pen moving, and trace out our continually lava-lamping mind.

INCANTATION NUMBER FIFTEEN
The Ragas of 2 p.m., 6 a.m. Mind

Us human mammals are hued by planet-turnings and the light-shifting cycles that shower down on our heads. In India (hallowed be its name!), there are musics—ragas—that are properly sung at one period of day or night, each with a different scale. How wise those Indians. Your body-mind will recognize which time immediately if you go by your neighborhood Indian music teacher and ask her to hum you the scales of midnight and dawn. You'll see what they mean.

TRY IT!

This one takes a day. You do other things in this day, your normal things of life, but as you slalom along, you write different slices as the sun streaks the sky. Maybe set it up on a day when the demands of the world will allow you to write at intervals along the whole journey of hours awake, here and there, at random samplings.

It starts when you wake up. It might even start before you go to sleep: you put out a call (if you do these kinds of things), a call to the dream world, a message: "I will write something tomorrow," and you go to sleep. Put your writing devices next to the bed.

And when you wake, it's simple: you write. Write from the mood and feeling of "just woke up." You might write from the man you met in your dream—how he felt, what he said. You might just emit streams of words. Whatever comes up—no thinking, no stopping—right away as soon as your eyes open. Nurture the poor creature of self with a lazy sleepy snuggly moment in your interior world. You may be writing *about* the dream, or you may be writing *with* the dream. Or if there was no dream, write with the state of mind you are in—delicious or grumpy, achey or spacey—whatever it is, write from it. But don't burden yourself with an "I've got to do this" mindstate.

When you finish writing, even if you only wrote for three minutes or so, you get up, you stretch maybe, get a glass of water or so. But don't go too far away; come back and look at the page. Circle a phrase or two that speaks of the dominant chord of this piece. It's your title, your key for this day.

Now what you will do is—as you stumble or glide through your day—you will let the hues of "day" wash over your mind. And every so often, pick up the writing again. Three minute write, and stay on the same theme. As you write, feel how the light slants through the window, through the leaves. Be aware of morningness, in whatever viscosity or translucency it presents itself to you. Let the quality of light and day sway what you feel. Noodle on it in the mode of 9:30 a.m. and of 11:15 p.m. Let the 2 p.m.-ness fully inflect what you have on your mind (cleaving still to your theme, held in the title). If the 2 p.m. mind denigrates and negates the sleepy 6:30 a.m., let it do so. Just stay true to the shiftings of your interior self. While you write, it's good to look out at the sky, the trees, and the sun in the shadows. Feel the quality of the air as the planet changes the scene.

Now say, if you are on a retreat, you could choose to do these extendedly—20 minutes at a burst—but I'll recommend something shorter, three minutes or five, and doing many of them, just because you want to make sure that you take a reading at every compass point and don't tucker out midway. For the real texture of the piece is the shift between the parts, the empty question marks that show the space between 4:45 p.m. and right after dinner. You're throwing a dab of paint on the canvas at each interstice in the day, and you want to do it all the way through to just before, "I am so exhausted, I am going to sleep."

You may not see what you are doing as you go. Not only is that OK, that's what we're after. What you want to do is write from within each space, not from outside of it. You want to be soaking in the infusion of the root-bark tannins of that mind. Tomorrow you can look at the finished work; tomorrow you can see what happened and learn. But if you are outside the process while you're doing it, that will hamper and subtract some of the essence of 8:45 p.m. and quarter to 11. A clue and a gargoyle could possibly get lost.

QUESTIONS FOR THE CURIOUS:

Is it tomorrow? Good. OK, here's the question: What did you not notice then that maybe you can now? What did you not perceive as words appeared on page that you can perceive re-reading it again? Can you recognize in the choice of "inflect" and "tucker" a certain stance, a certain take on the fluid medium of life-substance that you move in through your day? It's what we didn't see in the midst of process that hints at what we could.

THE MIND OF IT:

Cranky-groggy does exist in the same human person as ambitious and delicious. In some sense we kinda-sorta know this, but we take a pass on perceiving it as we hurtle through our days. An example! Ever send a pissy email late at night and regret it the morning after? Or write something swoony and moony under the influence of the stars, and then oh-my-god yourself with shame the next day after lunch? The tendency—or I'll say my tendency—is to give full credence to the logo-centric daytime office mind, and denigrate the musk. At least when I'm in it. On the other hand, all that busyness can feel completely bogus at the fresh cracked peppercorn of dawn. But the mind is valid. All parts of it. Guerilla warfare is won in the night. Skyscrapers are built in the day. And! Our perception of life is not just either-or; not just moony-swoony versus leveraged buyout. There's an infinite speckling of gray zones and color charts and spectral gradations in the arc of the day. These conjugations of mood make it slightly more or less probabilistic that your pen blurts "Zounds!" or "Gee willakers, Bob!" when expleting your spleen. The planet is turning and the solar winds rustle the leaves.

EXPERIMUNDO NUMBER SIXTEEN
Moved by the Muses of Visual Art

Every once in a while I get a call, sometimes an apologetic call, from a visual artist wanting to take a writing class. "I'm not really a writer, but . . ." And my heart breaks. Who did this? What dastardly person split visual artists from the artists of words?

In Japan, in the tradition of Zen-Ga, or Buddhist scroll paint-ing, words and picture-images were never separated, the poem and the image living happily and interacting as if this weren't a problem. We can use this insight, as always, as another route to "free."

TRY IT!

Like many of the techniques you've been meeting here in Sway, Moved by the Muses is an access point to a part of the mind's intricate and interior resonances that are as yet under-appreciated, and under-connected to the creating of words.

For this, you will want to get a passel of pictures to sway at your words. You need images with a particular feeling or two: a fruity pungency, or a narcotic hypnotism, or a sharp bracing bite. Best if you can scour up a variety. Many. Some old National Geographics work well. Take a photo of a redwood forest at dawn from this issue, a picture of Times Square at night from that. The African savanna, colonial Williamsburg, two small Cambodian children playing in the late afternoon sun.

Like a whiff . . . but with a picture

Or how about pulling art books down off the shelf? Raid all kinds of pictures: Marc Chagall here, Rembrandt there. Or you could use a single collection of Picasso's work, from youngest youth to very old age. Select one from each different period. Or maybe you are in the mood for disjunctive—a Monet here and a Robert Mapplethorpe there? Add in two African masks and three conceptual artists from the '50s. In any configuration, make sure you have enough of these pictures to feel the feeling "many." Too many is just right. Try to get images that are full and complex and indeterminate—not in the sense that you can't make out what they are (although you could try that too!)—but in the sense that they are evocative without being one-dimensional.

You could even do this in an art museum. Your sequence of pictures is your route through the halls. The guiding principle in all this is that the images resonate with you, that they promise something more than you see on first glance.

Here's how it works. You get together your imagery pile—however you've collected it— and you decide whether to preprogram the sequence or let it be random. However you do it, just be sure you don't have to think about it when you move to the next part.

Again you have a title, or theme, or idea—or steal one from an already existing piece. Take a thorny problem. Take an object from your "I want to write about" list. (You could make a new list every other day if you wanted to, or keep adding to the old one.) Take a freewrite you've done before with some other technique. Read it to yourself and connect your mind with what it feels like now. You're going to see it again, write it anew.

Is your pen ready? Your topic in mind? The gateways open? Ready to go. Now deal yourself an image, and when you start writing, you translate the piece through the language of the imagery, through the feeling of the shapes, the color as it enters into you. Let the image aromatherapize your mind.

See the thorny problem through the photo of the aluminum-paneled kitchen, or through the lemon-rind sorrow of the look on that woman's face. The trick is not to abandon the thing you want to write about *or* the sway of the image. This isn't "about" the art work. You are not doing art criticism, and it's not an exercise in using "precise descriptive details." See last generation's writing books if you want something like that.

You've got an image of Cambodian children. You are writing about your own difficult relationship with your singing voice. Do not let your default mind go, "Now what would the Cambodian children say about this issue?" or "They are so poor and I am worrying about such a bourgeois thing" or "I bet these children love to sing, and don't worry about being on pitch" or "They are oppressed by the violent government and don't sing at all." How to not let that happen?

The answer is to invite something else that is far more mystical and intriguing: it's to let the *feel* that you get from the image steer your mind, and infuse your being, and inform the pen. If you can be receptive to it, that "feel" is incredibly precise and shaded and nuanced (even if it is spicy or racy). That precision can deeply guide the piece. It has something to do with the way the slant of sunlight comes through onto the spotty grass behind those kids with a certain melancholy urgency.

As always, when you move to the next image, there's no padding or transition. Move through all the images you have, say five minutes or so each. Next, next, next.

THE MIND OF IT (FIRESIDE CHAT):

We miss aspects of this world, we lose track of them. That's one of the purposes of going to the theater, or looking at paintings, or reading important books. In your thorny problem, or stuck short story, or teaching issue with your kindergartners, or whatever topic it is, you have (wisely) given up the bulldozer "problem solving" approach. That is good. This technique is a reminder that the world is full of nourishment and freshnesses. Art is here for us to help stay connected. It was fired in an intensely hot crucible. You chose these images as guideposts— intuitively they moved you—and then you let them nudge, flex, and breathe you as you moved the pen through your piece.

Oscillate and Push Against: Pushing the Boundaries at the Edges of Your Work

Now why do children love swings so much? Go inside for a moment, to your memory of "swing." A time you really had fun. Feel the apex going back. That moment of suspension. You tuck your feet in and ooomph yourself down. Each oscillation brings you farther away from the stasis center. Each effort in one direction loosens the muscles and allows further extension in the other. Each alternation a "farther" to find. Each extremity . . . is a Push Against mind.

This chapter is something new: oscillations. A back and for-thing between poles.

"But waita minute," (you may say) "isn't Writing Open the Mind about going with the *flow*? It's about easing into things, right?"

Well, true, and in nearly twenty playplaces we have done that. And what we're doing here isn't the opposite of easing, but it is a way to use the tension energy of pushing against and swinging back and forth to help the mind surprise itself. Which is what we want.

The concept here is that by playing with the mind's tendency to push back, we can slip past the "possible" and squeak around the big bulky piece of furniture in your way and end up in the cup of incredible tenderness, or parallax or perception, without having to do all the long haul most of us think we have to do to get there.

EXPLORATIONALIZATION NUMBER SEVENTEEN
Wild and Stuffy

(Warning: This technique involves egging and goading!)

What is wild writing? Lots of cuss and swear words? A kind of rampage? Lewd? Screeching? Define it for yourself. And ask yourself, "If I were to write something irreversibly wild, what would it be? What instructions would I give myself?"

Would you *break the rules*? Be rude? Would your sixth-grade narrator take dissected frog parts and throw them on squealing sixth-grade girls? It is well said that "wild women don't get the blues." What wild do they do?

Make your little list of "wild" practices and policies. An annotated wilderness. A catalog of snorting boars and cussing whores.

How do you get wilder? By swinging back and then forth, just as you can clench a muscle in order to relax it. So that's what our Wild and Stuffy is. Those are our polarities. Our swing back and forth. They're gonna give us the width of the spectrum. The stretch marks and the proofreader's marks. The loan sharks and the Noah's arks. By oscillating back and forth, we create space in between and freedom at the edges.

With this one you could just write anything, but I'll recommend finding Something to Write About.

This time (why not?), try a topic different from what you Usually Write. How about biology? Even if you don't know from biology, write biology. The dispersal of species in forested mountain regions over the early Pleistocene. Even if you don't know the Pleistocene from plasticine. What if you wrote about sex like you never have before (and, for you, that might be with only hints and allusions.) What if you wrote about some ragingly alcoholic family with a mania for chess living in Barbados. What if?

the mind:
where the wild things are

Before we start, let me also, professorially, say something about stuffy. We used to hate "stuffy": the polysyllabic pomposity, the operationalizations of variables, the passive voiceover always ducking the blame, the insecure and baroque flourishes and flouncings to make oneself sound important. But now stuffy can be a tool, a permission to go farther. Allow yourself (on occasion) to get *exceeeeedingly* stuffy. Because the higher we swing, the swifter we whoosh, and the higher the next apex. Polarization stretches the limits.

TRY IT! (OR, THE CIRCUMSTANCES BY MEANS OF WHICH THE WRITER WILL EXPERIENCE THE AFOREMENTIONED "WILD AND STUFFY")

OK. We've got oscillation, and we've got a topic, and we've got the definitions of what wild is, what stuffy is. But we also want to let these parameters evolve themselves as you move through the piece.

We will go back and forth between the two, oscillate six times. Start with stuffy. Slide the wire rims down to the end of the nose, and look down with eyebrows arching up. "The writer shall begin by writing on chosen topic in 'Stuffy' manner for minutes four." Explicate carefully the theme under consideration. Speak genially of its nuances and aspect ratios. Adopt a thoroughly genteel air. Your countenance is cool, your manner precise. The timer is set. You have four minutes to pomp and to circumstance.

Suddenly!

Suddenly you go wild, you freaking freak! Put the pedal to the metal. Ride the white horse. The barrel over Niagara, the streaker, the football hooligan. Tear down the goalposts with a hoard of other screaming maniacs. Bark out commands. Screech and holler. Let the furor roar. Four minutes, no more.

Now back to the library and the small pinch of snuff, decorum and sanity, "enough is enough." The understatement, or the contrite soliloquy, the desideratum, not the fantasy. Four minutes.

And back! Ha haaa! You're horsemeat now sucker! Four minutes.

And back, "Thus, the upshot of our thorough analysis is decidedly such." Four minutes.

And again mud wrestling amid the writhing shameless hussies and the high stakes bingo grannies playing Russian roulette. Four minutes.

Oscillate, oscillate, wider and wider, to the furthest extremes. Each apogee-parabola-hyperbole on one end goads on the next. Watch what your mind does as it goes on its spree. Finish when you have your six chunks.

QUESTIONS FOR THE CURIOUS:

Well . . .which was easier? Which felt more natural to the right-now-you? (This will change: mood, time of day, ratio of dyspepsia to hallelujah, etc.) Did your writing (you can look at it now) in the less-easy-and-natural section, in the more trials-and-tribulations-for-you section, do something interesting by itself, without your intention?

And some other questions: When you swung back and forth, were there interpenetrations between offense and defense? Between Yin and Yang? Sumatra and Newfoundland? And how did the *content* spill over? How did the *feeling* spill over? Also, do you notice any difference between Stuffy one and Stuffy two, or between Wild two and Wild three?

THE MIND OF IT (AKA, DISQUISITION ON ABOVE TOPIC):

Different mindstates fertilize and intensify each other. Conjuring up the "stuffy" and plunking it right next to the "wild," and careening between them, back and forth, makes them leak and seep into each other's dominions. We get more wild than we could have if we brutally enforced "only wild" for a certain piece of writing. We also import some of the potency of all those big words and weighty concepts and grandiosity of stuffy into the stream of the wild. On the stuffy side, the wildness gives bite and storm to the pompous gut and pretentious clog.

Feeding the Width of the Spectrum

Another thing happens when you play in the territory of this wickety little construct called "stuffy": you can escape from the stockade of your own worry about what "academic" is. Ordinarily when we think about "academic," we put on our little strait jacket. All kinds of "No!"s start firing off every which way. A minefield. The problem with the internal voice that says, "Don't do it that way," is that it's *too damned fuzzy.* The "Don't do it that way" voice says, "That's too wordy." Or, "That's not professional," or "Is that turn of phrase too informal?" If what academic "is" and "is not" doesn't get defined, it seems to be everywhere, and is frightening: an ever-present Blue Meanie always ready to put you in your place.

If, however, you can get a handle on it, see that it behaves in this way, and not that, and doesn't jump out from the corridor all the time with its briefcase full of F minuses, then, when you play in the fields of that high-falutin' diction, it becomes baubly, kind of an interesting territory where you can chewing-gum around its mystery. We transform the "formal" into something new by saying, "This learned academic gurgle is another object, a tinker toy for us to tinker with." Why not liberate a phrase like "statistically insignificant" by glomming it on to "brouhaha"? Why not abrogate a sentence like, "Particularly useful is the concise survey of the foundational essays . . .," with "squeamish protoplasm" and some KY Jelly?

On the wild side, also, we find that we've been living too small. We thought wild was only dirty words, or epithets and expletives, but in fact it was monkey screechings and lice scratchings and warlock bellyachings and maniacal seed-saving, and long intense glares.

Who would have thought? Polarization is your friend.

RECAPTURING THE ORIGINAL SPIRIT
NUMBER EIGHTEEN
Observe-Abscond-Observe

Your friend asks you, "What's the name of that tree?" And though you know the name, you're not sure you want to tell her, because . . . because . . . you don't want to rob her of the experience of the tree's unique treeness by saying "Buckeye," because you *know* that most people are likely to use the label as a way to stop seeing the thing in itself. They say "OK! Now I know it's a buckeye. I understand." And the perception door closes. You don't want to *do* that to your friend. She's a nice person and you don't want to hurt her.

What ways are there to understand the tree? Your friend could be feeling the bark, closing her eyes and smelling the new leaves, putting the fuzzy blooms against her cheek, remembering its twig shape in winter and its cauli-florescence in summer. Now she's watching blooms turn to nuts. Now entering into the magic of light playing in its breezy boughs. But how is she gonna do any of that if her mind slams shut with, "Oh, *that's* a buckeye!"

Well, that's nice and neat, Andy, you might say. Now we understand, "naming is bad and wrong," and I won't do it because once I do I'll never experience anything again.

But, making use of the Law of the Infinite Revisability of Text,[1] I'd like to say that the opposite is also true. The name and the phylum and genus and class and the angiosperm and gymnosperm nomenclature for the tree can also be a way to spiral into the essence of this incredible being, "tree." Tree that is both spirit of the druids and raw materials for the Dixie cups. Tree that is a network of root hairs in co-evolutionary nexus with mycelium in the duff, as well as hard big thing to not smash into when you're skiing downhill. Naming and learning can send you away, but, handled deftly, it can also bring you back.

It's true that we live in the Age of Information. You can go to a reference book to find out anything. You can always go to a reference book. You want to know some facts, and the experts, they tell you. They tell you *sooooo* much.

But what happens to you? Deflation!

"Ohhhh," you say to yourself with a descending tone of despair, "everything anybody could say about this has *already been said*." People have written Ph.D. dissertations about the fluctuations in the migratory respiration wing-tip feathers of this bird and I didn't even know its *name*. "What use is there for a miniscule person like me in this vast and indifferent world?"

Your writing shaman:[2] "Don't do it!" Don't let the tumultuous ocean of facts puncture your desire to perceive. Revere your own holy sense perceptions and the magisterial imagination! And then add in the factoids and data tabulations. But do it on your own home turf. Abscond with their phraseology and put it in your snarky sentences and confabulations. To their scantron forms, add scalawags. Mix in a gremlin with their grammatological analysis. Take their "from a psychodynamic perspective, one might argue that. . ." and add in a "they stared deeply, painfully, dynamically, psychotically, into each other's eyes."

---

[1] I made that up.
[2] That's me.

OBSERVE–ABSCOND–OBSERVE ✦ 97

TRY IT!

In the grand kingdom of Oscillation, this is one of the principalities: Observe-Abscond-Observe. As in Wild and Stuffy before, we will use the power of going back and forth. Here's how:

You want to choose some item in the world on which you have a reference book nearby, but a reference book that you have not yet consulted on this particular thing. A painting in a museum, and you have an art history text book. A bird outside your window, and you have an Audubon guide. A psychological disorder in your housemate or your boss, and you have a diagnostical psychological reference guide. A national monument, and you have the guidebook to it. A historical building, and next to it is the interpretive plaque. A weed in your yard, and you have the Pagan-Wicca Guide to Medicinal Hullabaloo. A lightning storm, and you have Meteorology for Twelve Year Old Boys. The rigging on a tall ship, and you have the Boy Scouts Guide to Nautical Knots.

But Wait! *Don't* read that analysis yet. Just be sure you have it.

So once you've decided on your object of perception, your Thing in the World, what we will do is oscillate: writing about it without "knowing" it, but from your own inimitable perception—fully—then taking the tiniest little sippy-cup sip of factualities. And then move back to writing from what you yourself feel, in the perceptual realm, and also from the permission you get from your own imagination. You start with Observe. Look closely and intensely. Observe with your ring finger. Observe with your nostrils. Get down and intimate with this thing. If the object is the stars in the heaven, put your face up into them. If it's frogs in a green mucky pond, bring the sensory apparatus right down to an inch from the surface of the muck. And write.

Yes, you may describe. But don't be limited. Limited to "There are many many stars; they twinkle a lot." Not even limited to "Pinpricks of luminescence cascading their silvery light on my abject ignorance and awe." Describing is good and nice; metaphor is transcendent and blue. All of that is fine, and it's a good way to get started. But we want to go from description to imagination, to imagine ourselves into the interior of this object or being. Try to extract all the knowledge and understanding you can from your encounter with it, making free use of unsubstantiated supposition. Use the tools of careful looking and of irresponsible making things up. Push against all that you don't know about it, all that you wonder. Keep writing for a while, (seven minutes? you decide) then take a pause and a breath. Gaze off into space.

Now, in just a second, but not right yet, you will open your book of accumulated knowledge, your book of We Know This Because We've Studied It in University. But first: see how you have come to understand (through the writing) this painting/bird/psychological disorder/national monument/historic building/medicinal weed/storm/ship's rigging. See what your own internally-wise self knows. And now . . . turn to that Ocean of Facts, waves lapping at your door. Feel your internal changes and shifts as you transport your awareness to a different locale in the brain. Now read "about" this thing. "Learn" about it in your school kind of way. But *don't slack back into a mere receptacle of knowledge.* Don't read too much, don't fall into the Know-It-All's hypnosis. Stay alive, stay with your creativity, stay with the wide-eyed-with-wonder child's gaping "Look Mommy! The moon" mind. The child's "Did you know that Kangaroos live in *Australia*!!?" way of touching the world.

Get a few factualities, but just a few, and let the mind still be rife with the imagination. If the book says, "These unusual lizards may squirt a thin stream of blood from the corners of their eyes when frightened,"[3] let your imagination think of fear and blood and how they bamboozle each other. Ask your imagination what *usual* lizards do, and think also of eye corners, and of the loca-

[3] I did *not* make that one up! Herbert S. Zim, *Reptiles and Amphibians: a Guide to Familiar American Species: A Golden Nature Guide* (New York: Simon and Schuster, 1953.) (212 Species in Full Color! Really! I found this by total random. Believe me!)

tions for fear, and of how lizards remind you of gizzards and wizards. In short, engage the full and active and liberated and playful and ingenious mind. Don't forfeit that away to some meek part of yourself that says (like in the Bad Old Days) "I'm not worthy" and "I have to study for the big test on Monday."

If the *Dictionary of Art and Artists* says, "in the more limited context of modern art, the Expressionist movement may be said to spring from Van Gogh's use of drastically simplified outline and very strong color,"[4] even as you are reading, do not submit to learned-ism! Play in your mind. "Movement is springing from Van Gogh!" And your mind's ear hears, "Van Gogh is just *so* drastic!" And then you think, "Hey, and what is a drastic outline, and what is the limited context of color?"

So, the key is, don't read too much, just enough to trawl for a few burry nuggets, a little piece of brackish beachcomber bracken, like a girl on a nature treasure hunt with her little woven basket and twinkling eyes. Also! Don't copy anything down, just see what you see, and remember what you do, even wrongly. To remember correctly is not the point.

Now pendulum back to the crazy freewriting again, but this time pollinated with both the particulate matter of new wordings and the vibrational twangings coming from the mind-ways of the author. Let their world view (which they were certainly so very confident of) smudge up against your own way of seeing, but without it capsizing it.

Return, too, to The Thing Itself. Look and gaze again at the Object of Perception, (painting, frog, rigging, stars) and keep writing. Let the interpolation[5] begin! You are writing a crazy mixed-up soup, a regular minestrone, Rice-A-Roni alphabet soup of: 1) what was happening in the first burst of writing (you

[4] Peter and Linda Murray, *A Dictionary of Art and Artists* (New York: Penguin Reference Books R14, 1959.)

[5] **interpolate** *v.* ~transitive: 1. To insert or introduce between other elements or parts. To change or falsify a text (!) by introducing new or incorrect material. — *American Heritage Dictionary*

know, all that "touch it and insinuate yourself inside of it" stuff), *plus* 2) the crimped and curly edges of harvested data points and fact-checked opinionations from your Great Book of Knowledge, *plus* (this one important!) 3) whatever you can now perceive in glory of the Thing Itself *because* of your reading. Thus you will cycle and circle through Known, Guessed, and Seen.

You will do three bursts of writing with two readings in between. So write for a while, and then sneak back to the book for the tiniest bit. Then back to the freewrite, full screams ahead, for the third and last time. Three cycles of oscillate, between the felt world and Those That Wouldst Know It. Keep on reclaiming "your place, in the family of things."[6]

QUESTIONS FOR THE CURIOUS:

Maybe this time, *you* want to come up with some questions? Remember, all these techniques are experiments. What if you and your friend were sitting there and doing this exercise together by a rock covered by anemones in the bay? What would you ask him or her? What kinds of things would you like to know about his experience? Write those questions down. Now ask them to yourself, and see what your answers are.

So here are my questions: Did your mind shift with the acquisition of this "objective" knowledge? What changed? How was the feeling of your freewrite interpenetrated? Were you able to keep the thread of exploration and that rich inner world of guessing and imagination when you spiced it with facts?

THE MIND OF IT:

OK: here's where I show my hand. I'm mad. I'm mad that when I try to learn things, all of a sudden I become passive and abject and flattened. That I kowtow to Learned-ism, and I become an empty vessel awaiting their knowing knowledge.

---

[6] Mary Oliver said it like that.

Or I hear some official hypnotizer on the radio speaking about the *need* for a weapons system, and before I know it, I've been dumptrucked into their way of thinking. "A major threat to America's security, blah blah blah . . ."

the sense of not knowing:
mystery or agony?

And I think, How can I reclaim myself? Or even if the input channel is not so pernicious, like an auto repair manual with its intake manifolds, fan clutches, distributor caps, and tie rods, I soon find myself drowning in the prosaic. (Which is like the Passaic.)

So here's my answer: Let the carnies (with their facial scars and felony convictions) at that orderly office block of language. Take the world back with your glorious hallucinations. Grind the encyclopedia through the fun-house mirror. Recapture your excitement and wonder of being twelve years old. Did you want a pony when you were a little girl? What was in that imaginary world of you with a pony? That magic is always listening, lingering, waiting back in some corner, dusty and poorly lit, but nonetheless waiting, between the BTU's and the IRS. There it is.

Only to a magician is the world forever fluid,
infinitely mutable and eternally new.
Only he knows the secret of change. Only he knows truly that
all things are crouched in eagerness to become something else
and it is from this universal tension that he draws his power.

— Peter Beagle

So now here's the last mystical realm I wanna invite you into: the realm of "epistemology," which is just a fancy word for talking about different systems of knowing whether or not things are true.[7]

---

[7] Check me if I'm Wrong, all you epistemologists! I'm just borrowing your glamour.

And the cool thing is that *you've already been playing with it.*
Just now. Do we know lichen by crinkling our nose at it or by
weighing it in a mass spectrometer? Do we know where the
Apache people came from by really accepting the words of the
elders, "We have always been here. Here is the story: One day
coyote was . . ." or do we know by looking at a confidently-
drawn diagram with arrows showing Athapaskan language
groupings migrating across the Bering Land Bridge and spreading
out through the Yukon and south?

pulsating between ways of knowing

Each way of knowing has its own truth. Each one lets us into
a little of the vast mystery hoard of the world. Do not throw
away food at this smorgasbord. Do not kick over the table of
your gracious host! There are many ways to know. The philosophers think the people reading the pulp crime novels are degen-
erate. The biophysics people look down on the romantic poets.
The businesspeople think the philosophers are obtuse and full of
hooey. And all the adults smile smugly at the child who sees an
invisible friend. Everybody kicking over the table of their gracious, gracious host.

And this exercise is my one little mumble-humble answer to
this problem, this problem of how one way of knowing wants to
trump the other. Let's rub them all together, like herbes de
Provence. Let a thousand flowers boom.

IMPOSSIBLE REQUEST THE NEXT
Translate Natural Beings into Syllable Sounds

In the central Indian language of Telegu there are more than
four varieties of what we here in English lump together as simply
"r." The South African language of Xhosa has four different kinds

of clicks (full of meaning) to be found only in that language and nowhere else. Chinese, as is well known, expresses whole *worlds* of meaning through rising and falling tones.

Word sound has both texture and meaning, that is to say flavor and substance. We are so in the thrall of meaning that we forget the capacity of our physicality to create hisses and screech.

The word "meaning" itself has that *ee-ee-ee* in the middle. And hundreds of times a day when we are speaking we use the *eeee* without even a consciously-noticed thought. But there it is, our lips pulling back, sound resonating in the middle of the mouth.

What sounds occur in the throat when you try to express—gutturally, pre-verbally—the presence of an unripe apple on your backyard tree? Can you "get" that apple through syllable sound? And that little colony of mold on the refrigerator door rubber, what is the message it says in textural vocal elocution? What is the spoken translation of that knotted clump of seaweed, with its Gotham of flies? The shadow of that specific turkey vulture slashing across the dry grass: which inarticulate syllables, what murmurings and diphthongs would you use to express it? Not just "whoosh" (though you *could* start with that). How would you *replicate* it, create the same experience in words on paper that you had in your whole self when you experienced the wind blowing the shadow? What unexpectable words would they be? They may be odder than you think.

So what we'll be doing here is to use Push Against to do the impossible: write about something without using words. That means that we take an object in the world, a boulder, a puppy, and we give to it only inarticulate sound, the warble and splish of the physically-sensed world.

As usual the good purpose is to discover something new about your brain and the world. Something new about language. And to be free of subconscious restrictions on what you can do.

TRY IT!

Let us take a Thing of This World. Perhaps a shred of moss. Why not? Why do you need a redwood tree? A little pile of grass clippings. Or the fur on your dog. Something right there. The edge of the pond.

So place yourself in front of it, and look for a while. Now start writing gurgly, inchoate, no-word syllables. Your goal: to recreate that being, this little pile of grass in its entirety, by the sounds you write on the page: just letters of pure "meaningless" sound. (I *know* it's impossible; that's exactly why we're doing it. That's the very power of Push Against.) The trick comes from *continuing to do it*. Try four or five minutes. Or ten. Don't stop. Keep Pushing Against.

Here was me looking at some waves on a bay, from a staircase about 20 feet above:

waaawah sowwuhh showung shroongun wooop sissk sissk sissk sissk pladdle

Look at your little pile of grass, push your brain into it, and put letters down on the page. Keep moving the pen, keep looking at your Thing. Capture everything about it in letters on page: texture, color, its messages, its intention. You repeat letters and sounds. You try different kinds of letters and sounds, in different combinations, writing the sounds that looking at the being creates. This works best if you *keep going* and don't stop to "think." Hear the sounds as you write. Use the whole palette of sounds, and the back part of the brain. Let go of the logic. Not all waves are rolling "r"s. Try. Try again. Even as your brain says you can't, get it down on the page. So if someone read it, they'd say, "Oh yeah, that's a little pile of grass."

Ding! Timer up.

Here is the second part. (Finished the first, right?) Let out your breath. It's another freewrite in which you do it again, but you *also* use words, real words in English. *And* be infiltrated by the soundings, the guttural-izations and susurrations sloshing that you taught yourself in Round One. Also! Here's the permission part: the meaning of the words you write does not have to have *anything* to do with the object or being. Just words that contain or resonate with your sounds. They do not have to be recognized "words" in the Scrabble dictionary.

Here's what my bay waves sounded like:

strict packed pinched jumped clamped bunched chipped sapped
ripped cliffed jumped tamped tamped fished.
squaw squaw squaw crisp tamped
babble triple jimped sampled tamped dumped ripped

and then, when I was writing, suddenly, other words, surprising words, jumped in there too:

dramamine huddling single double mandible borscht drone

I do not know where they came from. That is the power of Push Against. If I hadn't pushed against, I would never have found dramamine *or* mandible. I would have given up, or gone literal.

And, lastly, before you start writing, here's one more permission (but let it happen by itself): if all of a sudden a sentence flies in, then you may bow to its imposition. A sentence that comes to you from wherever it comes. For me came this sentence:

A migration of camel backs. Cords ripple through the supple
musculature of ocean.

And then the freewriting subsided into syllable babble again: *palpation . . . priation . . . salivation.* Ah the great wonders of the powerful Push Against.

QUESTIONS FOR THE CURIOUS:

Did you sense a "push against"? Was there resistance in you? If so, good. That sometimes angsty friction can release some heat. I know it's impossible. (If you got mad at me for doing this to you, that's OK too.) And did a certain word come out that maybe might not have without the conjuration of syllable sound? Do you feel closer to your shred of moss, your pond, your pile of cut grass? How has your relationship changed through syllable sound? Keep trying this experiment again:[8] it keeps giving you the goods,[9] and each time in different ways.

THE MIND OF IT:

Once, in a great writing class, my teacher Leslie Kirk Campbell asked us all to imagine an ecosystem, a landscape, with its plants and animals, everything, but not to tell the other people in the class which one it was. Then we wrote down nonsense syllables for five minutes or so. And then we read. And guess what? Everyone could identify desert from rainforest from boreal coniferous forest from windy rocky island. No one got it wrong. We all knew.

Sound is connected to places and things, on a deep pre-human level. Language is not all about abstract thought, or even all about storytelling. Rock sounds like "rock." Your mind has a capacity to know a fern, a crag, via the intricate combination of your mouth, chest, tongue, lips, larynx, and soul. Give your pen that permission and you'll discover a capacity latent inside.

[8] Keep trying all of these experiments again.
[9] All of them keep giving you the goods.

Accordion

Already-written pieces have a tendency to become hard. Brittle. Solidified. Done. Or done-ish. Even a freewritten, *really* free freewrite becomes calcified.

Why is there a tendency for this to be so? Gravitational field? Perhaps it's like the way that the larger the planet, the greater it pulls on itself and the objects around it. The already-written text becomes a mass, a chunk, and it doesn't want to be changed.

But the mind itself . . . is fluid. Or it can be. I once heard someone quote someone else who said something like: "The human mind is both the most fluid and at the same time the most obdurate substance in the universe."

I personally am an advocate for fluid. "Yeah," you say, "me too!" Problem is, most people say the same: "I agree. Let's have a fluid mind." And yet, (comma) look around. Everyone all a-sayin', "Let's be free. Who's against that?" But *the next thing that comes outa their mouth* (and they're looking 'atcha right in the face) is incredibly rigid and Neanderthal. The mud is congealing and they can't see that they're stuck.

The most interesting thing about this phenomenon is that it only happens to other people. As for ourselves, yes, the mind is open and flexible and free. (Hah!)

So. Let's then redefine the problem: How can we get free when we don't know how we are not free?

The answer: Accordion!

What?

Exactly!

The not-free mind says, "We can't let go of this word, this paragraph, because it is *absolutely essential* to everything."

So what do we do? We throw it out. Then we put in its place something *utterly irrelevant,* and disconnected too. And we do it again. And again and again.[10]

Is that what this Accordion is? Yes. Accordion is taking away and putting back in. It is letting go of way way too much, far more than Control Meister would ever allow. We let go of lots of things we think that we need. We let go of control of the piece: it slips out and becomes fuzzier in focus, it skittles, it quakes. It's a loss and gain, and a loss and gain, a pulsing in and out.

The writing becomes new when we throw parts away. New parts flood in. Granted, the piece may change from wombat to kangaroo. But freedom . . . well, it means being free. Throw caution to the winds, three sheets to the wind.

TRY IT!

When the body breathes out, the lung cavity gets smaller, and then it fills up with different air. When a piece of writing breathes out, its quantity gets smaller and then appears something new. Again and again, new air comes into you, old stuff flies out. Accordion is an oscillation between minus and plus. And the breathing is deep. Expel all the air, breathe in big draughts, expel something else.

You start with something made: yours or someone else's. Take a short story or an essay or a freewrite or a rant. I like doing this with a newspaper article that upsets me.

So you read the piece and scan for phrases that interest you, or that affect you. Something chewy to pop with your gum. Underline these. Choose five phrases out and let them migrate to a clean white new blank page, no spaces between. The accordion is in.

---

[10] If this just freaks you out too much, then go ahead and tell yourself "I can put this part back in later." I give you permission, by the powers vested in me, to tell yourself, "I can put it back in later."

Set the timer. Ten minutes exactly, and let the accordion breathe out. In the new freewrite, you keep the same words in the same order, but you infiltrate new stuff (any stuff!) in between, rewriting the old phrases and letting new stuff flood in. You can stay on the same topic, or you can completely shift gears: shift genre or attitude or viewpoint or self. You have many techniques in your quiver by this point in the book: go any which way you like. Explanatory jargon or bardic odes may take up a new residence between the phrases, or a sleek slippered foot. Keep the pen moving until the timer goes Ding! And you cycle in again.

add and subtract, pulse in and pulse out

Oscillation back. The accordion does not stop. Take out five different new phrases from what you just wrote and recopy on a new page separate from the last. You have official approval from the Office of the Illuminated Scriptorium to let a few little smidgens of the original phrases and wordings from the very first piece lichen themselves through each cycle, surviving from one iteration to the next.

Now as soon as you have recopied the phrases, set the ten minute timer, fill it back out; breathe it anew. When the timer goes Ding, you accordion back in. Do four full oscillations as the tracery of the original recedes into soft blowing snow.

QUESTIONS FOR THE CURIOUS:

Hey, hold on a second. Don't rush on ahead. There is a tendency to skip the questions, to short-circuit the inquiry. While it is always the case in *Writing Open the Mind* that you should do everything you want and nothing you don't, at the same time, we don't want to miss *all* the scenery as it flings itself by. Right?

So here's some q's: Can you detect a slivery shard of the original in the last cycle through? An echo, a pulse? Beware of the gremlin that whispers seductively to you, "Of course there's nothing left there. It's just a totally different and new piece."

"Because, Sir Gremlin," (you reply), "Didst not each piece spring from the one prior? And even if not a single word remains, dost not the Etruscan pottery shard leave its evidence, its ghostly relics in the architecture of the particle accelerator?"

follow the tailwind as it snakes through the sky

Also, how differently did the cracks and gaps get filled in piece one than they did in piece four? What new shape did the piece take on and become? Can you now look back at piece one and see what is lurking, unseen, about to emerge and flower in cycle three or cycle four? If so, now think about the newspaper article from 1854, the essay for 10th grade English, your freewrite from last week. Maybe *all* writing is crouching in eagerness, waiting, wanting to thrust itself into the future, to become something else.

the world forever fluid ...
all things ... crouched in eagerness
to become something else
—Peter Beagle

THE MIND OF IT:

Well, for one, breathing is good. It keeps the flame burning at the temple of impermanence. Your mind is infinitely transmutable, and it helps if you tell it so. For two, essences may emerge in cycle three or cycle four that seemed like only little curlicues in life cycle one. An embellishment becomes a backbone. Words clothe themselves in different contexts and mutate. The bullies in the little girl's schoolyard transform into the bullies of Jurisprudence and the Office of Budgetary Management.[11] Other things can shift: a feeling stays with you but becomes something else. Sensible narratives can become vaguely creepy romps; political laments change with the strawberries and cream.

---

[11] This happened to me.

Accordion is a kind of mutiny. The traumatic event becomes a shaggy dog joke.

text is infinitely mutatious

In all of your writing (and everyone else's !), little words are linked to other words huddling somewhere off the page. They are in parking garages, Greyhound bus stations, bake sales, tramp steamers, bagel shops, and minimum security prisons for white collar crime. They have second cousins and brothers of great uncles all over the place . . . and we had no idea. Cut them loose from the fabric they're tangled in, and they link up in egalitarian rural communities to chop wood and carry water and make macramé.

And, of course, accordion is just good practice in throwing away.

there's plenty more where that came from!

And what your piece becomes during the process of Accordion tells you what you are capable of, and illustrates the currents of the imagination. If we don't see how far the body is capable of stretching, how can we know the proper amount and kind of movement it needs?

DEEPLY PENETRATING GAZE UNDER BUSHY EYEBROWS NUMBER TWENTY-ONE

Turn and Look Again; Turn and Look Again

Ever notice when you do something again, and then again and again, you tend to build up energy? Let us ignore for a moment that this energy is sometimes resistance . . . and just see it as energy. This time, we're going to *use* that power.

Doing something again and again is a rhythm: the repeating of words. The repeating of words. This "push against" can take you a long way. It is building energy through the friction of reiteration. When you push against your resistance, it's like re-asking yourself the same question again: it causes a "deeper," where your mind tells you to go. By restating, (not just using little ditto marks to indicate, but physically forming those same words again), you build up some pressure, and it must be released.

TRY IT!

We'll start this one with a face. Think of a face. A face you know well. You could love it or hate it, but you can see it in your mind. Write down the person's name at the top of the page.

A timer is needed, or a stop watch or clock. We will do three five-minute timed freewrites describing this face. Why not—you may ask—one fifteen-minute freewrite? Because then we lose the precious push against. Trust me, it's different.

See the face for a second before we start. A visual in your mind. Now set the timer and go. Write the nose, ears, and eyebrows, chinny-chin-chin. Short sentences, move on. If the furrows in the forehead say something, or metaphorize, jot that down too, but then rubberband back to the aspects of face. The first cycle is the key, so load it with details from the front and the side. Put down as much as possible in your limited time. (Be strict with the time.) The clock is also your friend: it forces you to get down as much as you can. Ding goes the bell . . . annnnnnd stop! Draw a line underneath.

Now this is where we go somewhere new. We're going to write it *again*, which is different than just adding completely new stuff. "You aren't asking me, Andy, to just copy the whole exact thing out word-for-word, right?" Yes, that's right: I'm not. It's somewhere in between copying exactly and adding something new. Actually recopying the exact words, and *a lot* of them, is what gets the goldfish around the linebackers.

So how much of old and how much of new?

Well, first answer is that you want to be sure you're getting that buzzy-staticy feeling inside that tells you that you are building up the energy. A guiding compass point might be 50 percent or even 60 percent of the words rewritten, again, same-same, and the rest can be new.

Here are some escape hatches:

1. You may re-order the words in freewrite two: they don't have to be in the same sequence.

2. You may allow the same words to have different meaning.

But you *do* write those words again. Quite a lot of them. Keep looking back at freewrite one. Feel the power of repetition in your body, and also the friction in your mind that says, "I'm writing the same thing again when I could be adding so much more!" The fiction that says, "I can't even write all the things I have in my mind because my hand won't move fast enough, and you want me to repeat what I *already said?*" Yes. Exactly. It does a new thing. That new thing will be good. So that's how you do freewrite number two. Five minutes. Exactly.

Now, three is the kicker. You rewrite it *again*. By now, you are slightly drugged by the repetition you've caused. Keep on writing, going back to freewrite one and freewrite two, recopying words from both of them again. Repeating words again. Repeating words again. Let the repetition annoy you. Let something break through. Keep watching what happens, but don't stop the pen. Five minutes . . . time's up.

QUESTIONS FOR THE CURIOUS (OR, YOUR FINDINGS?):

Did you discover anything about the relationship of *pushing* to what came out of your pen? Was there a distinct different feeling, or a different kind of wordings than came out with the flow mode from before? Can you make any grand statements about the way "push against" works?

THE MIND OF IT:

Words repeated become a rhythm. Sentences repeated create tension, a kinetic energy. The rhythm of repetition generates a friction. A friction of frustration. But we don't want to get to the bad old wrong mistake of Writer's Misery. We want to keep that good and pleasant "keep the pen moving" feeling and yet not lose the power of the slippery struggling fish sluicing around the linebackers. Because the effort of repetition is spring-loaded, it vaults that slipperiness into an unplannable place.

My own experience is that I drop down below the denotation of the words and I see things in a more metaphorical, more mysterious light. I understand this face, this human, this koan of a being in a way I had not before.

Why is this so?

Here is my speculation: I think it's a natural thing for the mind to fidget under redundancy. It chomps at the bit. It wants to break free, make new patterns. The mind cannot accept—the life force itself cannot accept—doing the same thing again and again. If, under this dissatisfaction, you then allow the mind to write *some* new words, a powerful energy is released, and the mind really takes that permission somewhere other than if it had just had free reign to write "whatever" for fifteen straight minutes.

The idea is that sometimes the words written under the yoke of "pushing against," in the "I don't *want* to, Mommy!" frame of mind come out in a strangely potent way, *because* of the pushing.

Also, because the mind is forced to repeat some words by the rules of this game, it tries to find new connectors to those words, to keep itself energized and interested, and that results in the mind being told by itself to find something different and other, a fish in the sky.

Architectures: Building Your Writing with Everyday Objects (and Some That Are Not)

Buildings. Makings of things, elaborate things, with passage-ways and heating ducts and conduits and struts and joists. Stacking things on top of each other with buttresses and flying archways and pedestrian overpasses. My question is, "Why do only tradespeople and architects get to do that stuff?"

And my answer is, "They don't." We can too. Now if you've read this far, you might imagine that *Writing Open the Mind* would have no truck with the Roman-numeralized structure of an outline, into which serious-faced young schoolchildren using slide rules fit pre-digested bits into pre-conceived nooks. And you'd be right.

But we still like to mess around placing things next to each other to see what happens. When the staff here at the Institute recently discussed this issue, it occurred to us that the intuitive, hodge-podge-lodge mind, the bat-on-a-hot-tin-roof mind need not be excluded from the multiple pleasures of putting larger things together. One of the researchers proposed that we could build a piece of writing by taking Symbolic Objects (like chicken wire and sponge cake) and putting them out on the floor, and adding in Key Phrases (like "the cup of friendship" and "the pursuit of happiness") and—with other as-yet unnamed objects—let them congregate, reorganize themselves, formulate a few grand theories and salsa picante, and then see what happens from there. Just for example.

Sometimes these "things" (river rocks, transistor radios) form different cliques and factions and shifting alliances, and the ad-hoc teams gather closer to one another (or snarl and grumble at each other) and become three-dimensional stage directions, or high-power antennas to complex feelings states, which then flavor and direct what comes out of the pen, giving all kinds of clues about what goes where and how they feel about their neighbors. These architectures, these funky structures of the internal babble and ponder, now brought out into the light, cultivate a more multi-faceted, nuanced set of attitudes, approaches, and ideas *because* of the support of the physicalized pattern of thought constructed in front of you. Sometimes the "parts" hold some more potent resonances for you. They might even be sacred. When they gather together, they create their own chanting, changing geodesic dome full of light, alive, in your interior.

Architectures can be built from inside to outside, or the other way around. We can take what we feel inside, all jumbled and cantankerous and portentous, and externalize that, put its pieces into symbolic objects, signs, pointers that recede back and pounce forward in order to figure out what is trying to emerge. Or we can start in the other direction, with the world that exists—parts and pieces of it—and let those numberless, numinous objects evoke and invoke complexities and potencies inside of us. We'll do it both ways. Read forward and see what I mean.

ROMPER ROOM NUMBER TWENTY-TWO
Gameboard[1]

Things are too complex to think about sometimes. Not without help at least. The brain can only hold about seven things in the front antechamber at one time. We get confused. We need to put things "out there," solid, on the floor, and see how they consort with each other.

Maybe your novel could go in any one of six directions. Where should it go? You turn it over and over again in your mind. Or you have a huge decision to make in your Life. Or "Why am I writing this book?" Or "Should I move to Chile?" Or perhaps it's just time to take a cross section of your life, on retreat. Whatever your question or topic is, it needs some architecture so that it can be thought about in space.

Imagine taking one of these sprawling octopi (above topics, that is), and convening all the outlying hamlets of it, all the pinecones and disavowed theories of it, all the locks of hair and totalizing meta-narratives and scars and racing tires all together into one spread to see what is attracted to whom, and how clottings aggregate and move.

That's what we're gonna do.

the ten thousand things

TRY IT!

This one needs space. I like a big clear carpet. Sitting on the floor invokes the child-play mind. Or you can use a table, but make sure it's big and clear of junk. Your game will be here.

words and cards

You'll need some things. All kinds of things. First of all pieces of paper. I just did this: I tore shreds of paper from a yel-

[1] Thanks to the brilliant idea from Julie Chen of Flying Fish Press, who exhibited her "bookwork" Personal Paradigms at the San Francisco Center for the Book, which gave me a few clues to start this with.

low legal pad, though I wish I had had some nice big index cards and colored felt-tip markers. But I didn't. And it worked anyway. If you're into craftsy things, you can decorate your cards with glitter and eyeliner. (If you're into Satanic ritual, use fur pelts and black nail polish.) You could even use chunks of wood that you can write on with a marker, or torn rags that will accept the pen. But what you'll need is something on which you can write words and short phrases. Lots of them.

On the index cards (or the pelts) start writing down words associated with this story or report or resumé or problem. "Trust." "Balloons." "Pregnancy." "Fred." "The raid on Harper's Ferry." And anything that comes up and you don't know why: "Trap door." "Ghostbusters." Also write down questions you have about the topic in general: "What is it about Chile?" "Can I get unemployment?" "What can we do about dangerous people?" Put each one on a different card.

arrows and things

Now also draw arrows. Pictures of arrows, on the cards. Plenty of 'em. One on each card. Curly arrows. Spiraling arrows. Lightning-strike arrows. Fat arrows and thin. A good bunch of double-headed arrows.

As you're going, you'll think of a new word here or there. In the play-place of mind, the subconscious bubbles up, like when you are on a walk, or changing a lightbulb. And then you think, "Lightbulb! Yes!" You suddenly stand up and get a lightbulb out of the drawer. A lightbulb to go on your Game Board! To be part of your collage. ("Are you talking about a *real* lightbulb, Andy, as part of the Game?" Yes. I am.)

Now you come back to the carpet and start writing *big* words down, one per card. Things like: "Spirit." "The Past." "Nature." "My Work." Now add in elements from your life: "Meditation." "Sleeplessness." "Phone calls from Dad." How about philosophical things and teachings from your teachers: "Set strong intention." "No blame." "The role of free will." A quote from the Dalai Lama. Or Willie Nelson. A phrase from a song you can't get out of your head.

When you ran into the kitchen to get the lightbulb—you now remember—you just happened to pass the spice rack. Now you think of it again. *The spice rack!* You run back in. Snag the bottle of curry (a metaphor in its yellow, powdery soul). Ginger. And sage. You know what *that* means (and it doesn't bother *you* that no one else in the world does).

externalize what's inside

Then you think, why not other kinds of food? You open the fridge and you're pulling out yogurt (culture!!) and next bananas (as in going!), and into the cabinets: noodles . . . and tea. Everything! What fun. An egg! Perfect. You bring them all back to the carpet. Put them here, put them there. Next you get into the idea of *signs*. As in, "It's a sign." A yield sign. You draw it onto a card. "Gas, food, and lodging." On another card. "Begin freeway." Sounds good. "Curve ahead." Then you think of that botched love affair. Curve ahead indeed! Write down *his* name on a card. Keep going. Then, suddenly you realize that you can do little drawings. Little bunny ears for that feeling so hard to express. Stick figures punching each other out. Childlike drawings: A picture of a house with a little puffing chimney. A little drawing of a snake. Your ex-boss! His name on a card.

Now you find that you are starting to arrange all the food and the arrows and the spices and the cards and the drawings and you see the connections, but you're also missing the . . . the . . . the something . . . Natural objects! That's *it*! You go outside and get a smooth river-worn stone from your deck, and you want to write a word on the stone. Nothing to write on it with? Try lipstick. And then, on the deck, there's a rusty gear, and a rotten garden glove. Bring 'em on in! Spread them out on the floor. No holding back. Make a literal mess. You can clean it up later.

Postcards! A confab of post cards, a bonanza of signs. Everything a symbol for something, everything invoking an aspect, a contending force, in life . . . or in the piece we are writing.

Now you're drawing little faces: different emotions on each. One per card, one per card. Go to the medicine cabinet. Pulling things out: the decongestant and the pain reliever. A sex toy? Why not? Put it next to the egg, or the curry powder. Or the sign that says Stop. Arranging already.

Bumper sticker slogans come to mind. You write them on cards. "Easy does it." "Just say no to hugs." "I'd rather be in the moment." "Alien on board."

You get the idea. Anything OK! Chants from your friendly neighborhood Marxist street protest, "The people, united, will never be defeated." Pick-up lines in bars. (Please enjoy writing. You owe it to me; I spent all this time writing this book for you.)

Write down a place name. Lisbon, Antigua, Wilshire Blvd. Draw some more arrows if you need them. Write down a feeling. Miserable. Electrified. Humble. Serene. Grab a tool from the workroom. A nail, needlenose pliers. It's your game board. You make up the parts. The metaphors abound. Toys from the toybox, little metal dumptrucks. The key is to have lots. Get many and many until you feel more than enough.

cohabitate and spar

Now, here's the snazzy part. Things start to group and consort. Lay out the pieces on the carpet and let them cohere and disperse. You may put one on top of the other; I give you permission. Things that feel distant? Move them apart. Are forces contending? Let them contend and compete. Create a spatial representation of the way things are: allow the complexity of the world. Use the arrows to create direction, narration, to indicate causation and the way these things move.

Important: Let the "meanings" of things shift as they will. Problem states can suddenly flip and become periods of incubation and nurturing. Festering truths all of sudden become hilarious

Punch-and-Judy klezmer orchestras. Gather clues to relationships as you are making this world. Gather clues by pointing arrows between "the past" and the bag of cashews. The yield sign goes next to the box of noodles. "Yield to the noodling," you think.

The clusters grow bigger. Nature next to community. No . . . wait . . .*under* it. Building whole architectures of relationship . . . until you feel, "Yes."

now to the pen

When you've completed your concoction, you start now to write. Write in a way that feels easy and lacking in rules. Don't feel obliged to explain anything, much less the mandala you've just created, as in, "This means *that* because it's next to the yogurt." Perhaps your Game Board turns into a "piece" itself, or direct instructions on what to write and how. Or maybe it gives you just the tiniest of a clue for the story you've been working on, and you run down the hall into another room and don't even *look* at the cacophony of monkey wrenches and pain killers and index cards spreading across the living room floor. Then, so ensnared by what was catalyzed that you fall into typing and typing, it's only when your housemate comes home and you hear his voice down the hall, "What the *hell* happened in here?" that you come out of your trance. (Just remind him that he's living with an Artist, and he knew that when he moved in, and keep typing ahead.)

Your only goal and intention in this game is to make something that "works" on you: shifts and changes the stuff in your mind, and to discover something about how you yourself work as a maker of Art.

QUESTIONS FOR THE CURIOUS:

Did you have a "Whoa, where did that come from?" experience? Did the questions you asked yourself shift their meaning in the process? Did the leftover pieces make their own tiny footnotery kind of comment or train of thought? (That happened to me.) Did certain things take on more weight and others less?

THE MIND OF IT (OR, THE REASON AND PURPOSE):

You can use this technique, this Game Board, to maneuver a manuscript into some kind of form. You can use it to watch the play of dust motes in the sun (the dust motes of your life). You can use this to figure out a problem that has never been solved. You can use it . . . as a game.

The appeal of the game,
the fascination that it exerts,
[is that] it becomes master of the player.
—Hans Georg Gadamer

The frame of mind "game" lightens the Serious, relieves the Importance. You become free of the Awesome Responsibility of the Artist. Games live in the same box with Silly Putty, slippery slides and Super-Elastic Bubble Plastic. That helps us get over the oppression of feeling that we're chiseling granite.

As in all games, you surrender to its purpose. The subject of the game is the game, not you . . . and this is a relief.

Play, by definition, gives you a new state of mind, which is what you were hoping for in the first place, picking up this book. And this new state of mind, of course, creates a different kind of writing (which, let's face it, is something that this hurting world needs).

One more thing about the way this can work: in thinking about writing, we have a hard time grappling with abstract forces like "relationship" or "influence." Sure we can write the word "heart attack," but how do we indicate how close or far it feels from the botched love affair or the booze?

In the end, the writing—simple words falling in sequence— must indicate the way things are. But the writer herself, in process, may need or want some armature, a metal framework on which a sculpture is molded, some experimental grounds in which to make use of the visual kinships and affinities that Game Board can give.

CONJURATION NUMBER TWENTY-THREE
Altar

An altar is an antenna to the mysterious force field of resonances that swirl about your trudging, dreaming, pondering, lilting self. It's a map of the psyche, in which you belong.[2]

Many things are altars that we don't recognize as altars. Places set up to become a particular mood, to prompt a certain mindspace, perhaps cause a certain kind of action to be more likely to occur. There's a little bookstore, Turtle Island Books, on a street near my house that carries only used and rare collectable books, old woodcuts and letterpress editions of books on the Arts and Crafts movement in architecture. Yes, as an arrangement of things, it was put in place to sell books. But I also see it as an invocation to the aesthetic, and thus the mindspace, of a 1930s world, a place where lithographs and Craftsman homes meet Modernist poets in first edition. You've smelled an old book: you know what I mean.

What about certain Cuban restaurants, with their yellow-and-red-and-black floors, walls, and ceilings? The chili peppers, the mambo music. That's an altar to a certain state of mind. In Mexico, on the Day of the Dead, people build altars with photos and objects, with shelves and cloths and food, with candy and candles. It creates something you cannot explain. Pagans build altars. Buddhists build altars. Catholics build altars. People put some things next to other things in order to create a place in the heart, to create a feeling that is exactly *this* way.

[2] There are certainly lots of ways of talking about altars that turn one type of person or another off. If you don't like the particular way I phrase it, bless you, and keep reading. If you don't think there is a Sacred, well, you can keep reading too, or just move to other parts of this book about Opening the Mind. I myself was raised as an atheist, so I should know.

The altar calls upon patterns in the world. Language is a set of patterns. Electricity and sunlight form patterns all the time, and, since you are an epiphenomenon of sunlight, there must be patterns in you. We can tap into these. People have tapped into them for centuries; they are hanging out there, in the ether, for us to connect to, like an electrical outlet, live, waiting in the woods. "Om nama shivaya." "Baruch atah Adonai, Elohaynu." "Jah! Rastafari!"

If you allow yourself to be changed,
what you write from that changed place, will be too.

There are things that hold power for you. A piece of jewelry. Your great-grandfather's watch. A particular stone. The reason they are in your home is because they connect to the contents of the psyche. And the contents of the psyche—as I am sure you are discovering in this kind of writing— are so numerous, so textured, disparate, and amazing.

In this exploration you will bring them out, symbolically, that is into physicality, and hitch your creativity machine to the bigger patterns, larger wave-forms ebbing through the field. Make this for yourself. Make it for your writing.

Your community might be in there. Your interior as well. Bring it out of yourself to show to yourself. Your altar will be a place that both represents and creates connection. You can not only identify with it, you can identify yourself in it.

There are three parts to this. One is a cultivation of a different feeling/energy state by putting that state out in the world. The second is basking in and receiving from that state. Third is then letting writing emit from that which has been cultivated.

TRY IT!

We're gonna build something again, like in our last adventure, Game Board, but this has a different feel. This time less wacky, more invocational. We're gonna put our heart in here . . . and why should we not?

It might be made in a clearing in the woods, a corner in your house, or smack there and huge in the middle of the garage. On your psyche's doorknob, place "Do not disturb."

Create a certain quality of energy, then let it create you.

Part One: Gathering and Making

Start by gathering things that have resonances for you. Walk around the house. Walk around the campsite. Take a photo out of your wallet. (You put it there because you love, love, love that person, right?) Keep gathering. What calls to you as you walk? What object or being in the physical world has a correspondent being inside your chest? A toy you've had since you were four. A small sketch a friend gave you. All things are symbols.

Now get something that makes light. Could be a gaudy fluorescent glow stick, or it could be a candle, a flashlight, or a pile of tangled-up Christmas lights. The soul responds to light. (This is a very ancient truth.) Fruit is also good: an offering, and—well, it's its own symbol, isn't it? It has ripeness and sweetness. You can put out little cups of fresh water if you like, and tiny bowls of rice. They do so in Laos, so how could we go wrong? Ask yourself, "What is it that's precious? What is it that I care about?"

Perhaps you are the type of person entranced by the high priestesses of Science,[3] capital S, and you worship its mysticism ("double blind!" "order of magnitude!"). Science brings you to a finely-felt place in your own mind. Then make your altar out of beakers, Bunsen burners, electron microscopes, and petri dishes; whatever gets you to the place where you want and need to be.

Stones and leaves, feathers and beads,
flowers, or images of hands, a rattle or drum
or a seed from a tree. A little lock of hair.

But don't use a single thing that doesn't matter to you.

---

[3] Some of the time, you are, aren'cha?

words

What kind of words are going on this altar? Well, maybe none. But we *could* put words there: a secret code language of your own, or something in Cyrillic or in classical Chinese. You could write a word in English on a torn piece of cardboard. Be true to yourself; it matters nothing what anyone else thinks about this. Make it into what you need it to be. You could put Wise Sayings. You could put that name that your darling calls you, or a prayer you made up. Maybe a phrase your dad used to say, or a nursery rhyme verse.

resonances borrowed from other times

Perhaps a postcard written by a relative now very long ago dead. Do everything you like, and nothing you don't.

theme

Do you want for your altar have to a theme? It doesn't need to, but it could. It could be "the sacred." It could be "the profane." It could be an altar to cars. It could be to your mother. An altar to writing, to writing itself. An altar to the people of Tibet, their freedom and peace. An altar asking for a friend who has cancer to be well. Something from them, something connected to them: their picture, a drawing, their name on a card. Well-wishing is good. It has its own extraordinary power, beyond its primary effect on others. A well-wishing for others, even unknown. "Grandfather, Grandmother, take care of the brothers and sisters on the road tonight. Let them be safe and not come to harm. Take care of them, Grandfather. Let them be safe."

sending energy back to relieve the suffering of the past
wishing well for a friend, or a stranger
praying for the repose of the dead

building

Now you start putting things together. How? Here's some structural stuff I've noticed about altars: they have levels and shelves. A higher and a below, piling up, fading farther into the background, coming out in front. Use space. Also, repetition is good. Repetition brings rhythm, connects parts together.

There are larger and smaller things. There are often photos of the living and photos of the dead. Sometimes a sacred substance. (Ink!) Deities, deities if you like: whomever you hold dear, for our purposes, is hereby a deity. Guardians: you are grateful for their benefactorhood in your life—the great English teacher in seventh grade who turned you on to words. Your therapist. Your mom.

And when your altar is ready, you can move to part two.

Part Two: Basking and Receiving

First feel your belonging in the altar you made. Can you find yourself there? And do a double check to see if there is something there that doesn't feel "you." You want to make this something that you can feel at home in. (Why shouldn't you have a sense of belonging in the world?)

Now connect in with your sincerity. Sincere energy flow out is like intention rippling on an oceanic swell. Ignite the lights on the altar and dim the lights in the house. Place yourself in front of the creation that came here through you. Try different locations to sit, closer and farther. Your body is at ease.

Create a certain quality of energy, then let it create you.

The second aspect is dropping down in. Let yourself gaze. "Gaze" is different than "look" or "see." It implies more time, a gentler focus, and a sinking in. Allow that soft focus (with your beautiful eyes) and begin to sink in. The imagination does its thing.

Part Three: Moving the Pen

Now take out the paper and pen, and begin to go in. Write whatever you want to, whatever comes up. Alternate gazing with writing, and then with gazing again. The writing goes in. And in and in and in.

THE MIND OF IT:

Putting things together in writing
is like building altars on paper.
—Adam Kinsey

Why is a room full of candles something? It is, though. With an altar you tune into a pattern that you recognize, and say "Yes," in a physical object sort of way, to your own capacity to be lured. Each part or piece of the altar has links to larger systems: a feather to a bird to a flock to the sky; a sacred phrase to the sutra to the whole book of prayers; images of saints to their teachings, their world. Quan Yin or Kokopelli or the Virgin of Guadeloupe: they have their specific resonances. These deities are ways of aligning our own energy dynamos to a particular flavor of being, and then sending that out.

A beating heart, a running athlete,
a dreaming baby, and a swimming fish
all generate electricity
just as surely as a power station does.
— "What Is Electricity?"
The Random House Encyclopedia

Is the altar ever finished? Is the writing ever finished? You could keep this altar moving. After pouring some energies through pen into paper, you could pull out some insights and put them on cards, paint them on stones, and put them on the shelf. Move the feathers and beakers and start your next journey in.

Prismatics: Faceting the Psyche to Gain Permission, Insight, and Surprise

Everyone's got a different stance. A take on this issue. On that. A two-cents to hurl at the world from the Grand Canyon vista point on life. Thing is, those stances in each individual, they shift; our intentions, they change. Little cabals of opinion makers move their think tanks around from one gristly corner of our skull to another, and set up a different bonfire here, a fresh one there. We forget one attitude or view or reason as we move on to the next. So, from the perspective of the free writer, the writer who wants to be free, when this exponential multiplicity gets underappreciated, when the gaggle of possibilities goes untapped as words flow from pen, what would be the holistic spirit-medium remedy? Another formulation of this question is, "What permissions to write newly could a collage of stances, voices, and intentions provide?"

Most of the time, the attitudes that snarl and flirt, the interior voices that idiosyncratically murmur or proclaim, or the divergent uses for writing itself are folded into some bland purpose like "making your key point." But then we are just recapitulating some statistical mean when we could be leaping from the balustrades and simultaneously whispering a sutra. So how can we prism these out? What way to let each member of the crowd get her turn at the podium without puréeing everything into a pre-digested mush?

One way is to make use of this basic fact: each internal attitude or voice or purpose has a physical location in the neurostructure of our brain. In Prismatics, we get access a number of different sectors, one after the other, and walk right into each of them with our hand outstretched and a welcoming smile upon our face. Then, each one, freed from the spider tangles of the others trying to stand on the center stage of awareness, gets its aria in the sun. That is to say, we will facet the ordinarily over-aggregated states of consciousness by the various vectors of attitudes, voices, and purposes, and let each be a different intention point from which to sprocket our investigations into writing and mind.

BABBLE NUMBER TWENTY-FOUR
Interior Voices in Contiguous Soliloquy

Ever find yourself using a turn of phrase only your mother uses? It stuck in your craw. The voices we've heard in this life have written a circuitry into our brain. "Four score and seven years ago." "I'll huff and I'll puff and I'll blow your house down." "And that's the way it is, I'm Walter Cronkite." "Can't we all just get along?"

Each of us was bathed in language for years before we started producing it. "Here you go cutie, open your mouth, the airplane's coming zooooom!" And, "What *happened*? Did you get an Owie?!" An ocean of language. All the sugar-sweetened cereal commercials. All the fights with your brother. All the Carly Simon lyrics. They lodge in there and pattern the brain. We are walking breathing ambling storehouses, archives, databanks of the kajillion books and magazines and speeches and chit chats that have passed through our ears and eyes. They jostle around as we saunter, and then, at some unexpected moment, you find yourself saying, "You *go* girl!" Or talking like your Uncle Allen, who lives in Nyeew Yawk.

Uncle Allen! Come to me now! Calling up the inner Carly Simon! Calling upon the Rodney Dangerfield. Speak through me now!

The conversations we hear become who we are.

Each one of us has a cast of *inner* characters as well, with different agendas and needs. A judge and a cynic, a sweetheart and a child. Some of them barge around like bullies, repeating themselves, desperate to be heard. And others are little billowy or skittery voices, in residence far at the back of the rare book room, waiting to be invited or coaxed to the fore.

The self is a plural, a context, a scene.

These voices are joined in turn by a society that chatters, roars in our ears.

But schools of writing, and our culture in general, tend to praise some voices and deny others. This often prevents us from writing in ways that feel true.

TRY IT!

OK, first to start, we want something to write about. Let's do it this way this time: "What I really want to say is _____ ." Try writing down exactly those words. Press the pen harder down when you write the word *want*. Then fill in that blank with a want. After you do that once, write it again, with something else in the blank. Try writing it four, six, seven times. Now choose the one you *really* want to write about, right now. Put that title or phrase at the top of a clean, blank page.

Now, put the journal or notebook down and take out some index cards or some small slips of paper or anything—the backs of old business cards—separable and small. On each write a name: Bob, the weird old man at the hardware store; your inner literary critic; Yosemite Sam; your ninth-grade English teacher.

The criterion? You must be able to hear or imagine their voice. You choose. Categories possible: cheesy pop stars, characters from your favorite children's books (*Anne of Green Gables?*), *family members!*

Or people who speak to you, Nelson Mandela, Mr. Rogers, Howard Cosell, people you don't even like (but you hear them), imaginary characters, classic movie actresses, Black Panther luminaries, your third boyfriend. You don't need to use only important people, not only nice people, not only *interesting* people—the wisdom you gain will come from the breadth with which you cast your imaginative net. Someone outright boring. Go on! Cast your net! Whomever you "hear." Put one name on each separate card.

If there's any inkling you *might* want to use a voice, write it on down. You have plenty of old business cards. Infinite. You won't be using all of them, so just create a massy messy hoard. A pile of voices in front of you now.

your own adult daughter
ten years after
you yourself have died

And let us not forget! The *inner* world, too, has voices. It's time to stop denying and get in touch with your inner cop. The inner soccer mom, the inner self-righteous college student, the sweetheart. Write them down. Use up those cards. You have *plenty!* The inner snob (welcome everybody to the table, no discrimination!), the addict, the wise sage (listing, listing!), the mystic, the schoolmarm, they're all in there. Hear, hear! The victim, the everybody-pleaser, the stiff upper lip. Everyone under one big tent.

So when you have cards aplenty, turn them all face up on the table in front of you.

Now look back at your topic. Just a glance. **O! Lovely cacophony!** Don't think too much. Now back to the spread of cards. Use the intuition and choose one voice to go first. Choose one that's easy to start with. This voice has something to say about what you really want to write about.

Now choose another voice. It has something different to say. But, optimally, it's not a simple opposite. Kind of slant. Juxtapose one smack against the other. Choose five voices, ones that you can hear right now. Put them in a row, a sequence, a one-two-three-four-five that's intriguing to you, that interests you.

So when you've got your voices in order, your ducks in a row, put the little stack of them face down in a pile in front of you. Clear the others away. They are yours to use for the next time you do this.

Take up your page again. Look at the topic, and . . . pull the first card! Place it in front of you. And let that voice speak. Stay with the topic, write in that voice: the words, the way of speaking, the opinions—let them bogart the steering wheel. It's not you. Don't stop to think, don't second guess or double take or hiccup or guffaw: just plunge ahead. Four or five minutes per voice, move to the next one. ("Next!") How would they say it? Hear them say it, move your pen. No padding or transition, just move to the next voice. Go through to the end.

Let a thousand flowers boom!

QUESTIONS FOR THE CURIOUS (INQUIRY SOUP):

Here's a different way to notice: Did you feel a certain space between the voices? Go back to your writing, and now read just a part of it. Read the end part of "voice three" and the beginning of "voice four" now, out loud, to yourself. Feel the space between the two. What does the mind suppose and figure and hypothe-size about that gap? There's a wondering. What is that wondering, for you? Where does the wind blow, between Anne of Green Gables, the inner football jock, and the wise woman inside?

Usually, in most "get to the point"-oriented writing, the possible possibilities may be left ambiguous for a while, but eventually, one by one, the other options are foreclosed and we come up with the One True Meaning. ("Anne of Green Gables represents a golden childhood, the jock is a bully, and the wise woman makes it all better in the end," or some such . . .) But what if it never *does* get definitive? What if the numerous possible interpretations of this collage are all still equally possible, and the story just keeps moving on? What is that like on the mind? To not *know* for all and forever and for certain, but to just leave it hanging?

Well, for me, I see it as *generous*. With this way of writing, many ideas remain in potential: options are not all closed down. See this for a fact yourself in your own work. The linkages between what voice Three said and what voice Four spoke are multiplicitous. Also lots. And thus . . . fun. So, fun plays with vaporous plays with darkly mysterious and funky. How can that *not* be good? Lo! Your writing isn't all declarative like a government report. Full and replete.

So back to the questions: Did you learn anything from these clamoring people? Did they speak amongst themselves?

THE MIND OF IT:

Reality is not one, but many. How can we reconcile the view of the world held by the Dalai Lama and that held by Louis Armstrong or Groucho Marx? Is one of them wrong? Have *you* found a unified field theory of the cosmos and why people act like that in the supermarket? Does it fit with the way you spoke things in the night to your high school sweetheart?

the multiplicity of the real world
via voices that inter-write us

Parts of Reality are incommensurate with each other—that is to say, incapable of being weighed or tape-measured by the same scale. So what to do? Just bail out and cling to a Great Big Theory given to you by God or Freud or Betty Boop? Problem is that even Betty Boop can't explain why people act like that in the supermarket.

So that's what this technique is about. We can have all the commentators weigh in, speak their babble, get in trouble. The important thing is to have each voice get its say. Since each of these voices was made by Reality (as you were), each holds a slice of it, a cross section at least.

Death to the Grand Narratives!
Long live the million small stories!

Also! One more cool thing. Very cool thing. You listen to these voices, but you aren't exactly calling up Louis Armstrong on his cell phone and asking him to talk on topic X, are you? No. It's . . . pause, hushed breath in the auditorium . . . in your own head! You are consorting with the multiple inner intelligences of the voices inside of you.

All of those voices you heard in the yard as a child, and at work today, and in the stuffy lecture hall: each one carved and sharpened and physically sculpted the brain sluices. And each voice in this world was sculpted itself during its days spent, centuries ago, in the mouths of the speakers of Old Norse and Finno-Ugrian, the Hamitics and the Indus valley civilizations— the words hucked and chipped, burnished and bruised. Saint Augustine and the Philistines: they moved words (the ancestors of your words) around in their mouths, and flung them out loud. And this language with all its vast heraldry was handed all the way down—one momma to one baby, one babble at a time—to your friend, to your brother, to Walter Mitty, to Pablo Neruda, to you, to your brain. There it is now, ready to speak.

IGNITION NUMBER TWENTY-FIVE
A Tinderbox of Attitudes

"Mommy, he started it!" . . . is an attitude toward life. It's a perspective. And a valid one. One of many. "Let's look at this reasonably" is another. But we miss perspectives driving down the Highway of Life. Or we forget them. Then we stumble upon them again, by accident, on the busy street, ("What's your take on this, Bill?") or in a crazy person who calls us on the phone ("The Devil is going to get you!").

These perspectives, slants on real life, what are they? They are permissions. Permissions to see things a certain way, to speak from a point of view. Take this one: "I am a glorious shining example of all that is good about the human race." Now who's gonna give themselves permission to speak from that place? But nonetheless, every once in a while, we feel it.

Tender stances.
Irate stances.
Naive stances.

We say, "She's got an attitude." In fact, that is good. We need attitudes. Lots of them: "I'm not your mother," or "I'm in control," or "It's not fair!"[1] All of these are aspects of real life we usually forget when we're writing. We miss the vista points as we speed down the road. This time around I'm gonna toss out a hailstorm of attitudes, like a batting machine, and you're gonna smack at them, one after the other.

[1] Children's voices are perfect for this because they learn to communicate these basic, undiluted human passions and approaches to the world, ones that become covered-over by truisms, polite abstentions, filligree, upgrades, new and improved features. But underneath this the child's tantrum mind, or pure "I wanna" mind, or pure cuddly mind can reconnect us to the substrata of our drives.

TRY IT!

Again, topicality. You are writing a particular character in your story, perhaps, and you can't get her right. Have her stop in to the vintage clothing store, or the changing room at Lord and Taylor's. Have her try on a buncha attitudes. See which fit.

Or, you just cannot figure out (and you've really been thinking it over) whether to move or not. Or whether to go back to school. Or whether to stick out your job which you hate for two more years to get the benefits. Or not.

And we can tell *stories* too; we're not limited to topics. Stories of my first pregnancy. Or someone I love has gone insane. Or we met an orphan girl on an Indian train platform. Or the story of my massive love affair. Or I was blinded in one eye by a cougar attack. (*Whoa*, where did that one come from, Andy? Don't ask me, call the subconscious complaint line.)

Or perhaps just invite the mercurial goddess of chance in, and just open the newspaper, find a headline, and write about that. You could even steal a topic from an English teacher or a text book. They seem to have plenty. It's against my religion to give you assignments.

Here's how it works. On the next page, I've got a cauldron of stances, a gumbo of attitudes, a library of slants. Each has a number. Once you've got your title, you choose seven random numbers between one and forty six in any random order, and write them down just under your title, like this "31, 11, 42, 2, 5, 24, 46." (No peeking first!) At first you start writing, any which way, for a minute or three, and then, go through your number list and write from each attitude for about four minutes each.

Got your numbers? Let's go.

1. "Evil is present in this world, and we must battle it!"
2. "There is no answer to this puzzle."
3. "I feel an incredible peaceful feeling in my heart just now."
4. "You don't know what you're talking about!"
5. Just leave it as it is.
6. *Disagree with what you just wrote*
7. "We have angered the gods."
8. "It's *capitalism* that's the problem!"
9. "Follow your bliss."
10. "Mommy, he started it."
11. "Do nothing, and everything will be done."
12. "Hush little baby, don't you cry, Momma's gonna sing you a lullaby."
13. "There was nothing I could do about it."
14. "A pox on both of their houses!"
15. "But I thought he was a *nice* man."
16. "The possibilities are endless!"
17. "I've heard it all before."
18. *Disagree with what you just wrote*
19. "It's society's fault."
20. "Do that some *more*. I like it!"
21. "No pain, no gain!"
22. "The timing was wrong."
23. "I *know* I'm right!"
24. "The wise would disapprove."

25. "If only things were different!"
26. "Let's look at this in more detail."
27. "If it ain't broke, don't fix it."
28. "It isn't *about* you."
29. "It'll never work!"
30. "Mommy, can I have more, *please!*"
31. "You poor *thing!*"
32. *Disagree with what you just wrote*
33. "She was doing the best she could."
34. "That's it. I've had it. I'm madder than hell and I'm not gonna take it anymore."
35. "You can't just throw money at the problem."
36. "My decision is final."
37. "I didn't want to say this, but you are forcing me . . ."
38. "We've forgotten to look at things in the long term."
39. "It's not *fair!*"
40. "The universe is in control and we need to just let it do its thing."
41. "Mark my words . . ."
42. "Like I'm *so* sure!"
43. "It's all my fault."
44. "We've got to have some *standards* here!"
45. "I am a shining example of all that is beautiful in this world."
46. "Let's party!"

QUESTIONS FOR THE CURIOUS:

It's all about surprise. Trying to get something you didn't expect. So the question is, did you get Surprise? Did you discover an inner attitude you had left out in the cold?

Also, were there attitudes you fit with better than others? Was anger easier than tenderness? Was there relief in some stances? Did you feel a release in your poor strictured soul when someone finally allowed you to be a brat? Did you give yourself permission to lie?

THE MIND OF IT:

Oh, the boundaries we live under! What a trip that we don't see them until someone says, "Look! You don't have to do it that way. You can be tender." Nihilism too has its place at the table. *And* I can be pathetic. *And* I can be righteous. *And* I can be distanced and austere. I can blame others. I can blame myself.

The prismatic psyche emerges through plenteous permissions.

There is not only the relief of being able to see sides of the issue or story that our habit-ridden brain had preemptively foreclosed, but the sheer multiplicity of possible approaches opens our relationship with the real world. Our relationship with the world is funny. Our relationship with the world is tragic. It's reasoned. There is an end to things. There is no end to things. (Yes, yes, logically speaking only one of two opposite statements can be true. But isn't it exhausting to always have to throw yourself at the locked prison door of logic? Isn't that your forehead with all those bruise marks on it?)

These askance-y stances, each one fits into a niche in the environment—the environment of your inner self, and the environment of the big fat culture, our being with others. They are niches for us to use; let us use them.

KALEIDOSCOPE NUMBER TWENTY-SIX

Seeing through the Prism of the Multi-purpose Mind

An old man once said to me—my Old Man in fact—"Son, the purpose of writing is to *communicate!*" Being full of the disrespect for authority he so carefully instilled in me, I disagreed . . . disagreed in that very California way with a "Yes, and . . ." (and not a "Yes, but . . ."). How sad, I said, if writing only had one purpose. *Pobrecito* writing! Poor sad little thing! But lo! It's not true! There are hedge-your-bets purposes and slam-down-the-fist purposes. There are public purposes and there are private purposes. There are exploratory purposes and shy, tickly purposes. We write to instruct; we write for revenge. We write to fantasize; we write to figure out. Each of these are different writing selves, and each of them need the OK to blurt what they know. And each one has, at one time or another, been shut out, closed down.

The question this time is: How does writing shift under intentions? What don't you know about your topic that shifting the azimuth of purpose could maybe reveal?

TRY IT!

Say, this time you could try using something *old* of yours to call up your theme. Something you've already got. Choose maybe something dug up from an archaic journal. You haven't looked at this piece in *forever*. Or maybe an article that you wrote for the high school newspaper. What if you're still in high school? A story from fourth grade then! Or maybe it's something more recently "old," something you have to write for work and you can't get it right. Anything waiting in the wings, ready to come out.

Or if nothing is ready, choose a theme that is new. This particular house of mirrors isn't dependent on the topic being an old one or a new one. Either way, what we want is a theme, and we're ready to go.

So, first write a word or phrase for your thematic at the top of the page. We'll write this in bursts. Start with your basic burger freewrite just to get the brain corpuscles firing, moving on the page. And then each next part is a shift, a change in your navigational bearings, to set your sights for a completely different shore (purpose-wise) while staying with your theme. Ancient mariners used to use a tool called a sextant to navigate the high seas: it has all these protractor-like notches and marks for angles of star and sea and horizon, and circles within circles. This technique is your sextant. I'll give you some bearings. You swing the pointer all over the map. Each burst there's a different purpose: you keep homing to your topic but change your reason to write. Three minutes each. When you are ready to start, look at the next page.

START!
Start vamping on your topic just to build
up some steam. (Three minutes.)
shift
Write to convince others.
(Three minutes . . . and don't read ahead . . .)
shift
Write to satisfy yourself! (Three minutes.)
shift
Write to represent a patent lie as
something that's true. (Three minutes.)
shift
Write to connect people to each other.
(Three minutes.)
shift
Write to vent and to dump your feelings!
(Three minutes.)
shift
Write to teach others, and explain.
(Three minutes.)
shift
Write to "do" something in your writing that
is forbidden, immoral, and wrong that you would
never do in real life. (Three minutes.)
STOP!

QUESTIONS FOR THE CURIOUS:

When you get free from the inarticulate (but stranglehold-ing) voice that says, "You've gotta write for *this* reason and not that," what are you able to write that before you were not?

I'll tell you a story about my own experience with this exer-cise. I had been teaching this technique for some months and then (startle!) a student in the class said, "What about writing with the purpose of connecting people to each other?" In that instant I experienced my own "Whoa!" moment, seeing that I had completely ignored that goal, not only in the exercise, but in writing itself for all these years. And why *can't* writing be like that? I thought to myself, "It *is* glorious for us to be in the company of each other, and to use writing to bring that out." And when I then wrote from that newly-glimpsed intention, I was able to write with a softer, more caring, more connected touch. A permission was granted, and I realized that I had not been free.

So in this technique you are saying, "It's OK." You're saying "Yes, you *can* write only to please yourself." And, "Go ahead! Selfishly dump the emotions on the page." And, "Now you can be as didactic and know-it-all as you want." There is no one saying, "That's a little bossy isn't it, Dearie?" or, "But I would never actually *do* that, never actually kick him in the head."

So the question here is, Was there a surprise point for you? Think back and see if you can catch the tail of that "unexpected!" moment. Can you re-enter the instant of surprise? Because that's where your power spot is, in the potency of your mind. If you can get to the instant that ignited the surprise, if you can *know* its texture, then it's easier and easier to enter it the next time you write. That surprise point produces the goods, again and again. Knowing it will help you more than twenty manuals of style. The deep mind is wise.

THE MIND OF IT (WHAT I'VE NOTICED):

It's true that we may "know" that there are different reasons to write, know on the "if you ask me, I'll tell you" level, but have we ever really delineated them? Ever asked them to play by themselves for a while just to see what happens?

the map *creates* the territory

These different goal centers in the brain, some of 'em are probably more ancient than the invention of vertebrates: "Get food!" "Please self!" Others more heady, recent: "Explore territory." "Find new idea." Or, "Help other critters for altruistic and goodly purposes." Once we disaggregate each of these centers and realize how spaghetti-tangled they had been before, we can give each of them a little bit of center stage. We have nothing to lose but "The way it's supposed to be."

Shaking up the Curmudgeon: Writing from the Kinetic Body

> Within this fathom-long body ... is contained the world
>
> —*Gautama Buddha*

Words come out of our bodies, and our bodies respond to words. The more attention we give to this spiraling circuit, the more vividly it plays out on the stage of our awareness.

Do you feel a certain way after standing in line? A certain different way rolling down a grassy hill? Do you feel a certain way after creeping along the hallway to sneak up on someone? Different again after playing horsey on the floor with your little niece? If the mind is in the body—and all of them scientists[1] tell us that it is—where is language? In the elbows? Well, actually . . . yes. A quadrillion tiny tentacles of nerve cells, suffusing the body, reaching out to the provincial outposts of heart, finger, and heel. It's all one conundrum, and electrical impulses shoot back and forth. Memories, words, feelings, all are intertwined with sinew and tendon and gut wrench and belly soft. The laboratories of the

Much of this great work I've developed in partnership with and learning from the dancer and actor John Chung. Good and gracious thanks.
[1] Important scientists

official officializers have proven this. Language is in the physicality itself. And that's important for writing.

Here's a fer instance: What if you were to turn off all the lights and then try walking around the house? I mean *all* the lights, so you can't see a single thing, and then begin to walk purposefully around the house. How would you write about breaking up with your boyfriend differently after that? It is the absolute case that moving the body moves the mind. We get to a different place, and getting the mind to a different place is what this book is about.

"But why use the body to find new places in writing?" the curmudgeon[2] might say. "I mean, come on, writing is *cerebral*! You think, and then you write. You think, and then you write. Closed loop. Case closed."

"Well, hey," says the jester,[3] "Yeah, it's probably true, you are unfamiliar with this way of working (poor grumpapuss). But since you're not dead yet, let's try something new!"

We writers are shy though. We don't want to phase-shift to moving around the room. Our culture has taught us to dislike standing up. We have shame about movement. We have been disciplined, afraid of "the ridiculous." We sit there, preferring motionless angst, tasting our testiness, more dirt clod than person, more bent out of shape than in. But the *body* is wise. It knows you need to move. Yes, you've heard "Go outside and take a walk when you've got a crimp in the brain," but why stop there?

And yes, I know, you are reading this in a book, and you're probably sitting. What a phase change to move onto the floor! But I'm pretty sure you can pull it off. People bend keys and lift cars with their minds.

[2] the curmudgeon camping on your shoulder
[3] other shoulder

RUBBER BAND NUMBER TWENTY-SEVEN
Rustling Up
Energy Textures

Imagine that there is a an unknown, uncharted place in which you have been invited to travel, a place jam-packed with hidden treatises on What's What. These treatises are camping out in crevices, obscurantized from view. They might be wisdom, or facts, or the story you will write, or the turn of phrase that you need. They are crumpled up little bits of paper on What You Know (but don't know you know) and they are scattered throughout this land.

This uncharted place is, in fact, your body. It can produce different textures of energy—sensuously silky, or deeply quiet, or madhouse gonzo—which can give you access to writing that you had no idea you had. The crumpled up notes get unfolded, and you can smooth them out, pressing them flat against your thigh, and read what they say.

TRY IT!

Let's start with writing about a Something. Maybe you write about difficulties with your parents. Maybe about adoption. Maybe about why you get cranky. Maybe about the elderly characters in the story who meet again at a wedding, forty years after those times when they hung out on a street corner as teenagers in Philadelphia. Maybe you have no "topic" and you just open to what happens. Any which way: good.

What's gonna happen is, by moving the body you will dislodge what you know, dislodge it from the cranky musculature that holds it.

So you need a space to work in that's yours. Could be the forest glade where you are camping, or your hotel room in a hot tropical country, or it could be some high-end dance studio, or it could be the living room with the orange shag carpet. A larger place with room to move around is preferable, but not demandatory. Somewhere your own, for the minutes we'll use. *A place where you can be autonomous.* That's what you need.

a temporary autonomous zone

We'll be doing writing and then moving and then writing and then moving. So before each movement texture, read that section—up to the next subheading—and then put the book down and try that kind of movement. And then come back to the page and write from that new space you are in. I've written each section in the present tense, as if your dear friend is reading it to you. (And perhaps she is!)

begin

First we'll begin to write, just to rev up the pen, any way at all, from sitting wherever you are, just to establish a baseline of wherever your body-mind finds itself in this particular moment. You can write on a topic if you have one.

just walk

After five minutes, you can put the pen and paper down, and,

gently with yourself—

just

get up.

(Watch the interior as you do.)

So, begin to simply walk; begin to move, just walking around. As you move through the space, notice things around you and let your eyes take them in. Shapes, colors, objects, lights. Now as you move you can begin turning, walking a different way. First do whatever impels you: shake a foot, turn the neck. Try walking now a little slower, now a little faster, and now take a direction that is not what you expect. Allow an impulse to carry you into movement before your conscious mind becomes aware of it. Pivot. Accelerate, then stop. Walk a little bit swervy, walk a little bit chunky. Bring your energy up. Walk, stop, and walk.

Don't do anything you don't like, but keep the energies moving. A little faster, a little more unpredictable.

An attitude of experimentation and openness pervades.

Allow your energy level to rise and . . . when you notice a shift, a shift in the way you are feeling, stay with it for just a little bit, then suddenly sit down, and put pen on the paper, and move it on the page. You may feel herky-jerky; you may feel flushed. Whatever the energy tone, write directly from that, direct that energy right into the pen, and don't stop to pause. If you are writing on a topic, stay on that topic. (If you need to absolutely, you can write *about* what just happened, but don't miss out on writing simply *from* that new state.) *Keep the pen moving* no matter what you may feel—just let the next word happen, then the word after that. See what occurs. Try this new thing. Write five minutes or so, then put down the pen, and move to the next.

stretch the rubber envelope

Now this is phase three. You get up again, and start walking the room. Walk naturally and easily first. No need to "do" anything. We're exploring this further, expanding the palette of movements. Let your awareness shift to one part of your body more as you walk: become aware of the pelvis, now the shoulder, now the jaw, now the tongue. Now move as if your body were being led forward gently by a string attached to the top of your head. Now attached to your ankle. Now to your belly. Now to your earlobe. Now to your chin. You can even crawl and roll if you want to. (Don't if you don't.) Feel the full expanse of the spectrum: stretch the rubber envelope.

And now allow yourself to drop down into an energy state of fluidity and grace, but continue to move. Move effortlessly, move gently, suffused now with ease. Explore the sensations inside this movement dimension: thick honey stretching down off the spoon. Take up as much space as you want. You can explore the floor, and different ways of relating to it. The knees can make contact with the floor, as can your side, your shoulder. You are fluidity itself. Drop into this.

And when you reach a shift in yourself . . . sit right down to write. Not a moment in between: move the pen on the page at any speed that comes. Let it move at the speed of your mind, whatever that is. If you have a topic, stay with it. Short time, five minutes, and Stop.

soothe

So again, one more time: a different energy texture. Stand up, walk for twenty seconds or so just to jiggle things out of yourself. And now . . . quite gently . . . lay yourself on the floor. Let the floor support you. Let the mind stay alert, but let the muscles release, soften, quiet down. And scan the body now, releasing, and notice how your body is. Also notice any areas that could release further, be more spacious, more open, be supported with more breath. Just notice those places and ask your body, with a sense of curiosity, "If those places were to release, how would my body feel?" Just hold the question without demanding an answer.

Notice your feet. Let them relax. Let them contact the floor, feeling the points of support from the floor. Imagine that your feet are sponges, soaking up warm soothing liquid. Why not be soothed? Let yourself be soothed. And follow on up into the ankles. The calves, the shins. Say "ahhhhh," in your mind. You are actually relaxing, saying a "Yes" softly to yourself, to each part of the body, slowly on up, seeping the warm liquid into you, up to the head. Really try it. It *is* good. Say to yourself, "Hey, I *want* to relax." Stay alert. Stay soft.

Now roll onto your side—move smoothly, move directly, right to the waiting page. Five minutes, and you're done. And now, how about, for a second, getting up, walking away, breathing air, chewing a mint, and then coming back to see what you've done.

QUESTIONS FOR THE CURIOUS:

Maybe this is *the very first time* you've ever done something like this. Wow. You didn't freak out and say, "This is Ridiculous." Wow.

Now look, wide-eyed and curious, at what ye hast wrought. Look at the four pieces and look for their differences. What words did you use in one state that you didn't in the next? How would you express the difference? Look at the pieces themselves and try to shift focus from the mindstate that wrote them, and see just the words. How did they change?

THE MIND OF IT:

Freedom is breaking away from the rules you've been telling yourself. If you tell yourself, "I'm not that type of person to skitter and sway, I'm too old, I'm too this, I'm too that," then you are obeying the dictum of What Is Not Allowed. The answer to this is, of course, play, and Rustling Up Energy Textures is just the beginning, the taster test to try. Let's continue and see the articulations of energy qualities that your physicality still has in store.

INCARNATION NUMBER TWENTY-EIGHT
Corporeal Antenna

This cycle of play, we're refining the shapes of movement: creepy movement, bossy movement, kitty movement. We're going from flour, sugar, and eggs to baked Alaska and crème brûlée. It's a further definition of the shapes and energies of movement: more fully-flowered, the meadow; more richly hued, the canvas.

Wander like a sheep, loiter like a drug dealer, reshelve like a librarian, saunter like a vixen. Do so, and the images appear on the screen of your mind, and—you'd be surprised—not just the obvious ones. You send these intentions, these shapes to the body, and memories come up. Wordings come up. Cadences and flavorings appear.

In the last cycle, Rustling Up Energy Textures, what we did could be described—roughly—as "fast," "slow," and "stop." But the repertoire of the body cannot be reduced down to just these three.

just the tip of the ice cream cone

We have stalker or bouncer; we've got delicate or jittery; we've got molasses or puma. These shapings of movement give us entry into precise interior points—and the potency of such access points may indeed be why wise Native peoples dance wolf and elk, moon and wind.

Believe it! There is information in the way your darling juts out her tummy when walking, information in how that tenth-grade girl sneers her lip, chewing her gum, smacking it loudly. Information in the movements of a chubby-armed infant, rolling her eyes, information in the movements of a very aged woman, tiny, stepping down the street. Information? Images, wisdom, sensation: the whole tomato.

Which of these knows the True truth of the world? Manic pedestrians in rush hour or sleep-walking raccoons ambling toward a dumpster?

All of them live in you

Moving in Corporeal Antenna is establishing an understanding, not just an idea. From the understanding will come language, unexpected, unexpectable. Each form is a collection, a precise, specific collection, of movements, postures, and gestures that become a gateway: you are teaching yourself. Let us not assume we know what the pedestrians or raccoons have to say before they've said it; let us not stereotypically predict what your friend Barbara would say about our topic just from thinking of her from our thinking heads, without moving in her shape. What we'll do here is enter into five different embodied shapes, which will be situations or attitudes or stances or people. I'll be providing full invocations and inductions. Let yourself enter as fully as you can into each.

This time through, there'll be two parts. First round I'll be guiding you, and then, after that, if you want to do this one again you'll have a box of toys to pull from yourself.

In this sampler I'll give you a mix of different types of shapes: a person, a being from nature, a situation that contains an intention. When you try them on, remember this is not "you." You are just taking on the Shape in the service of Art.

role is not self

Also, when you move in each form, invite yourself to move beyond the caricature of it. Sincerity is good.

TRY IT!

This shows you something hidden[4]—something you know but until now you've thought about only from the brain. I'll guide you through an invocation and, once you've felt that shape live in your self, its own particular quality intensifying, you move directly to writing. As in the previous experiment, you want to keep the waveform unbroken by going from movement to writing without a cranny for the thinky-think mind to barge in.

Oh, and the topic. Corporeal Antenna gives you a new view on something. Perhaps it's a story or poem or essay or something you are "revising." You could read it out loud to yourself, or parts of it out loud, before you start. You could even read a letter someone sent to you that you want to reply to. If you want to use this to draft something new, you could jot down a short list of points, ideas, and feelings about this something before you start. You'll want to riff on these words in your mind as you move through these shapes.

[4] As usual!

A few things to remember about moving: The floor exists. Use the up-and-down dimension as well. And side-to-sideness. And leaning. You are not shackled into being a vertical biped: you were made for more than that.

So do you have that autonomous space, no distractions, no one peeking? You're ready to start.

warming

Warming up is moving. Moving is good for the body. The body was designed to move. You instruct your mind to move the body, and the body, thankful, gives back to the mind. And once you're warm, you will start to take on different energy shapes while you continue to hold your topic, the piece, the questions, in your mind. There will be five energy shapes. If you are working alone, you'll want to read yourself one segment, try it, then write. Then move to the next shape.

Here we go:

shape one

As you are walking, think of someone you know *really* well. Perhaps someone you care about. You can see them. You can see the way they walk. Now begin slowly, gently taking on their way of walking. Their hips. How do they hold their hips? Keep walking around the space. Now become aware of their head and their neck. How do they move? What kind of steps do they take? Note any of the particularities and idiosyncrasies of their movement that you can remember, which make them uniquely them. Their belly. The gait, the way the toes point out or in. Their face—what expression? As you picture them, you take on their full shape and form.

Keep thinking about what you are writing about.

Think about what you like about them (maybe you even love this person) and hold that in your mind, vibrantly. Their *shoulders.* Can you start to feel the shift?

When you feel it, get a strong sense of the state you are in now: you will use this as a template to return to as you are writing. Keep the continuity of energy moving and go directly to your page. The movement flows from body right into pen. Write about the chosen theme but stay inside the feeling of the shape that you now know.

do it more

Write for seven minutes or so and move to the next.

shape two

Now gently stand up. Shake out the curmudgeon. Roll the head. Roll the body. Use the fact of the floor. Try moving on your back and on your knees and side and belly. And once you are feeling that you are indeed a Homo Sapiens—designed with full capacities to Do Stuff—you move to the next Energy Shape, which . . . is . . . Puppy!

Your mind says, "Hiiiiii! Great to see you! I like you! Will you play with me? Let's play *now*. I'm here now and and and and . . ." You *are* the puppy. The whole kaboodle is in *motion*. Butt—tail—paws—head: irrepressible. The world is good and you are in it. Sniffing, shaking, give yourself to it. Nothing is going to stop you. Uncontrolled. Moving fast (keeping the topic in mind) paws and tail. *Clumsy!* Full of yourself and full of Life. Give yourself over to this and, with a solid hit on what this state is ("got it"), move to your page. Write for seven minutes. Move to the next.

shape three

So find yourself standing up again. Something different will happen. Different is good. Shake off the old state. Be open to the new. Try using the word "release" in your mind. Walk around the space. Now see that you are going about your way on a sunny summer day, outside, walking down the sidewalk. Suddenly you see in front of you a little girl running toward you. You recognize her: *It's your cousin's kid.* You love that girl. She's running, oblivious, like a child does, and you see (everything now in slow motion as you are walking toward her) . . . the stick . . . "Watch out!" you think . . . *trip!* . . . You see her knee scrape, hard, on the concrete. "Oww!!" . . . a wave comes over you, "Poor *Thing!*"

You run up, and she's crying. "It's an Owie!" Squat down, looking at her, and feel the wave of empathy. Find the way you respond. The tears, the dirt in the wound. You are there; she's screaming. You comfort her. Put your whole self into that. Squatting down in front of her—you respond even as she squirms in her screaming. You clean the wound; she cries *more*. You try to calm her. Stroke her head. Comfort her. What is the expression on your face? Exaggerate it. Enter into that state completely. (Still, in the back of your mind, you are not losing your topic.) You make the smallest movements with the greatest tenderness. She is calming down. It is because of your love. "It's OK, sweetheart. It's OK." Bring this into your whole body. Your fingers brush her hair out of her eyes, behind her ears. Hold her. Hold what you hold dear. Move directly to the page. Write your words. Write for seven minutes.

Now move to the next.

shape four

Now you must fully shed the last and move to the next. Again walk around the space. Feel your muscles and bones. Move in different ways. Use your body in a different way. Now you are a . . . a . . . *monster*. A big one. You are let loose in a city. God-*Zilla!* You are destructive. Your whole being *is* destruction. The expression on your face: "I *will* dominate everything." This is your attitude; this is your shape. You are walking. Huge strides. "You will fear me!" You smash everything. Nothing is safe. Your claws pick up cars, your feet kick through shipyards and storefronts. You leave rubble in your path. "I will dominate you, and this, and him, and that, and . . . " Dominate with your hips. Dominate with your feet, with the whites of your knuckles. "I will rule and command. I will humiliate and humble everything and everybody around me." You own it all. You are bigger than life. Nothing is safe. Write on your theme.

and shape five

Completely abandon the last one. It sheds off your back. It drops from your bones. After the storm, the fresh light of day. Walking around the space, look up and around. Swing your arms and open your mouth. Let the new movement cleanse the palette of your mind.

This is the last cycle through. Hold on to your theme. Recognize the ground at your feet. You are outside in the salty air by the sea, at the shore. Coming over the sand dune you see the expanse of the ocean. "My god it is huge!" You move down to the shore; there are waves after waves. You walk into the sea and then . . . you *become* one of those waves. A wave rolling in. (You are not standing up.) Give your whole self to Wave. Now intensify the movement, the rolling of waves. Hear the sound in your bones. Say to yourself, "I roll in from the sea . . . in to the shore . . . up on the beach . . . foam to the peak . . . roll back to sea . . ." Again and again (thinking of theme) you are rolling to shore. Your movements are fluid. Your body is all water. Let it take over your mind. Wash up on the page. Write till the end.

(There's an expansion on this, a deluxe version, for the next time you try it—but if this is your first go through you can skip right ahead and question the mind.)

TRY IT AGAIN! (THE DELUXE VERSION)

It's Your Box of Toys

So you love this Corporal Antenna thing, and you want to explore all its hinterlands. Well, I have indeed a big box of toys for you, and you get to rummage through them and try out the ones you like. It's a box of Energy Shapes, and you get to choose ones you like, ones that intrigue, ones that promise to tell you something you do not yet know. Some are dollies, others Lincoln

Toy Box 'o' Shapes for You

(Pick and Choose in Your Inimitable Way)

Intentions
creeping up on someone
gathering berries
pogo sticking
kung fu fighting

Somebodies
someone you love
the cop in your town
your estranged sibling
your cat
your sibling
teenager
baby
geezer

Attitudes
"I yearn for everything"
"I want to care for you,
    and you, and you"
"No! No you can't!"
"Please! Mommy, Please"
"Anosher Drink! . . . Jusshh
    one moah drink!"
"I've gotta have it"
"I'm so sorry, so deeply sorry"

Moving with . . .
childlike curiosity
ease and confidence
anguished writhing
vast ambition
startled jumpiness
desperate grovelling
big-hearted sweetness
delicacy and obligingness
shy mincing steps

Moving like . . .
broken glass
fire
aluminum foil
plastic
spandex
ooze
ice

Postures
crouched
expanded
brittle
all muscles tense

Natural beings
waterfall
lizard
mana ray
volcano
high cirrus cloud
a skittery squirrel
deer in the woods
monkey
storm cloud

Archetypal characters
bouncer
vixen
amoeba/blob
hero
judge
boss
swami
villain

logs, little tin drummers, circuit boards with little bulbed transistors, stuffed bunnies, squirt guns, whoopie cushions, et al. You get to dig through it and play with the ones you want to.

role is not self

Try a variety—try three or five at a time. If you have a penchant for randomness, close your eyes and stab the point of your Bowie knife at the book. Or maybe look through with curious intuition and choose several, and then put a bunch of the ones you like on index cards (going beyond "liking" when you choose which ones), mix them up, and randomly pick three from the pile. Or use the cards to set up a sequence in advance. (The sequence we just did was: Someone you care about; A puppy; Comforting an injured child; Godzilla the monster; A wave on the shore.) Experiment with a sequence that pleases you, as well as one that feels different from the direction you would usually take. Or perhaps even choose some shapes that are the opposite of what you "want" to happen, and then be stricken by Surprise.

let the new state
speak (instead of your thoughts about it)
onto the page

Once you've got your series of Shapes, the process is first to read an existing piece of writing, or choose a theme/title/story. Jot down a few key words to hold in your mind. Then move around an open space and loosen up the bod. Take on the shape of that being, state, or attitude, and after each, write from that new state of mind, one burst of writing after each different shape.

Coupla things: take enough time to really invoke each one. Let its characteristic take you over, and you surrender to it. There's a point you get to where there is a shift. You want to get to that shift. Also, you want to start gently, and move further and further in. That's another way of saying, *intensify the shape*, whatever it is. If you are putting the movement shapes on cards, you could give yourself short elaborations in key words at the bottom of the cards, like above with Scary Monster: "destructive . . . dominate . . . smash . . . rule and command . . . nothing is safe."

And lastly, notice that each kind of shape has a lot of different nuances—specific nuances that you can adjust and fill in.

You are the maestro. OK: ready, set, go.

QUESTIONS FOR THE CURIOUS:

There's a continuum of ways that these energy shapes can affect the writing. The puppy can take over the whole piece, dictating all the words and the content as well as the feeling and the rhythm. On the other end, you could let only the faintest redolence of puppyness—hardly even detectable—linger at the outside edges, translucently, like a far skyline seen through a wall of glass brick, or like the brush stroke techniques inherited from Rembrandt, passed down generation after generation, might be deduced by an art historian, at a distance of centuries, looking at Van Gogh's *Starry Night*.

Look back at your piece now. How much of the obvious content of your energy shape penetrated into the final product? Could a person who did not know how you produced these five pieces tell which one was snookered by Godzilla and which one by Wave? There is no correct way to do this, of course. Try both ends of this continuum and points in between. Try it different ways at different times. Slide along the spectrum. Try full influence one time, and minimal the next.

THE MIND OF IT:

In these experiences, what happens changes each time, even with the same shapes in the same order. That's why I like this work: it's a shifting set of games, baffles, and self-hoodwinkings that never gets old. This time, if you want to think about this

"The Mind of It," I'll suggest that you go back and re-read (Ahh, the pleasures of re-reading!) what I wrote at the beginning when I was trying to con you into trying this work, before you had experienced it with your own physical corporeality. Read the introductions to this chapter and to Corporeal Antenna again and see what feels true there, and how you may "know" differently now that the body has been invoked as a site for understanding.

BALL OF CLAY NUMBER TWENTY-NINE
Sculpt Yourself into Your Own Words

Your body is malleable (being, as it is, made of clay). It has this extraordinary capacity, an ability called *gesture*. Gesture can take you a long way. Throw up your hands. Tip your hat. Do-si-do. In India (Have you been there? You must!) there are gestures you will never find here. Mexico, Italy—they speak with their hands. Gestures symbolize things: they *are* language. And like good language, each one can hold the meaning of a number of *different* things. One-to-one correspondences soon get kaput. Gestures have another niftiness too: not only do they show meanings to others, they create them in the gesturer herself. Make a gesture, and images flood to mind.

In our last set of experiments and messings around, we asked the body to take on intentions and positions that represented interior states, or people in the world, and then let language arise from those physicalized intentions, attitudes, and moods: yearning, brittle, a skittery squirrel. In this one, we're gonna let our own words—shreds and snatches from an existing piece of writing—specifically shape a physical language in our body, a series of gestures. And then we'll let that flow back into fresh language on the page.

So let's mess with this a bit. Let's switcheroo the word "ges-ture" for the word "sculpture." Because sculptures you can sculpt. You can sculpt them precisely. Like what if you were to embody a phrase from your writing symbolically (not literally) such as "the boys looked at us mysteriously" or "the bravado of East Trenton"? You wouldn't be directly explaining, but exploring something latent or sideways within the words. The part of the psyche that shows you your dreams, how would it respond?

> Words suggest gesture . . .
> shape causing imagery to appear in the mind . . .
> those images flow to words . . .
> spilling off the page.

TRY IT!

Take some piece of writing that has come from you—the title of your book, or a curious phrase—and write it down at the top of the page. Once I tried doing this with "Writing Open the Mind." I learned a lot I did not know. Choose any phrase. A phrase that catches at you: "I wish Dad were here." Something small: four or six or ten words. We will make it into a sculpture that moves.

So when you've got your phrase chosen and written down, warm up the muscles and stretch the rubber of your body. (The warm-up in Rustling Up Energy Textures is good.) Is it as easy for you now to roll over as it is to twist around backwards look-ing down? Move with your ankle or earlobe leading, as easy as pie. Each movement should feel available to you. That's good.

So you will start in a place, perhaps standing up, perhaps on your belly on the floor (probably not in a chair), and you say your phrase once out loud. And say it again one "piece" at a time. "I wish," then "Dad," and then "were here." For each part, a word or two, you make a shape that symbolizes that word, an image in space, that communicates this word or short phrase. Try to go for the sideways interpretation; don't short-change the metaphor. Avoid one-plus-one-equals-two. Avoid the greeting-card version.

Here's how I learned this myself: Once, in a group full of sculptors,[5] I was sculpted by someone else as "anarchism." I was expecting a caricatured image, some gritted-teeth, bottle-of-gasoline-chucking pose. The good thing was the surprise: one arm, palm up, near my cheekily cocked head, eyes puckishly diagonally up, my other heel off the ground, shoulder rolled back, wry smile, hip out. There! I learned something new—I was successfully un-duped.

So now for your words; you want to give nuance to your shape. Use the curl of your fingers, the tilt of your eyebrows, the angle of your hip. Why bother being shy? The power of sculpting works less when you hold yourself back. Give yourself to it, commit to this word-sculpt like you commit to your writing. Maybe you are lying on your back with your legs in the air. Maybe you have one knee on the carpet and your mouth open and your torso bent around to the right.

Urge yourself beyond the obvious. You need allegory, obliqueness. The predictable isn't bad, it just isn't *enough*. First thought is good. It may not make "sense."

Now cycle through the sequence again, the same shapes but now with more precision and care. Any gesture will do, of course, but the fine filaments—the exact curl of lip, the twist of the wrist—make for a more exact feel: and it's the exactness of feel that creates the imagery and sensation in the body in just the right way.

Here's the next part. You've gone through this twice. Now you do it again, but this time make the gestures much smaller, and do them in a row. "I wish . . . Dad . . . were here": shape then shape then shape. Now go through them again, the slightest possible movement, barely moving at all. Now the last time you do it, do it just in the mind. No outward movement at all. If some-

---

[5] Give great good thanks and praises to Augusto Boal, progenitor of *Theater of the Oppressed*, where I learned the concept of sculpting. This is incredible work. I suggest you do seek it out.

one were looking at you, they wouldn't see the slightest movement as you go through. You've transmuted the energy, taken it inside.

Now go direct to the page and write down the phrase exactly as it was. Now whatever else comes. A five minute burst.

energy changing shape,
on Earth as it is in Heaven.

QUESTIONS FOR THE CURIOUS:

If some disbeliever were to ask you the following questions, how would you reply? "Why would making a gesture for 'daddy' teach you anything you didn't already know? What different words would physicalizing 'I wish' into a fully knuckled, twisted, prostrated, gripping depiction produce? How would any of it be different from just sitting there in the chair and writing on the topic of 'I wish Dad were here'?" What would you say?

THE MIND OF IT:

Well, this would be my answer, if any disbeliever were to ask: It has to do with what I said at the beginning of this chapter, that the mind is actually located in the body, the nerve cells filigreed all over the hip, tongue, and thigh. So when you hold the body in a sculpted place—"the bravado of East Trenton" or "the boys looked at us mysteriously"—there's an organic, pre-verbal knowing that happens, and from that knowing, different kinds of associations happen—visual associations in imagery, emotional resonances, certain palpating or dirge-like cadences. All of these can transform into words, and those words will be different than before. Because the mind is in the body. In it. Animals communicate primarily in gesture. And we are animals. We translate an open-armed gesture into meaning just as we translate a bristling dog with teeth set, or a bird tilting her head this way and that, into communicated language, something we recognize.

Automatic Writing from the Interior Terrarium

I don't know if you've noticed this, but we've been awfully bossy with the body. "Move to this word and that! Shake and gesture like a platypus! Like broken glass! Like a neurotic! A snail!"

What a lout we've been. You can blame it on me.

So the body itself, what does it want to do? How would it tic and blip if it weren't charged with Transmuting a Theme, with figuring out why your boyfriend does that? How would it ooze and burble if it didn't have a concept at the controls? What words would it put into the pen if it were allowed to just move by itself? So far, you told the body what you wanted it to do, and then wrote in response. Now let's just *allow* the body to prompt us, listen to a sensation—whatever sensation is there—and then respond to, feel, and intensify it, and let writing flow from that.

TRY IT!

Isn't it nice to return to No Purpose? We need more of that in this country. They should pass a law.

All you need for Interior Terrarium is your pen and journal, and a clear piece of floor. No mood, no stance, no approach, no theory, no god. Your human-given body and some space. You don't have a topic, you don't have a theme. No idea or story or problem or plan.

Since this is an eyes-closed one, you'll want to read this through first, then hold the sequence of steps in your mind so you don't have to go to the book as you move through the phases.

So, the floor. You lie right down. Put the pen and paper off to the side, nearby. Close your eyes; feel the points of contact of your body with the floor. Take a breath, and then, listen . . . listen to the inside—you know, the *physical* inside. Notice heart and breath first, you have that . . . *there*. Now look for a feeling, a sensation, a twitch, or a giggle anywhere in your body—calf, hip, shoulder, palm. How does it present itself to you? Whatever the sensation—itch or throb or yearning stretch—you observe it, and you let it prompt you to move. It might start with a turning of the toes, or it may be a side-to-side of the rib cage. The body leads, and you follow its moves. It may tell you to tremble, it may urge you to curl. No judgement, no analysis—let it evolve in whatever direction it seems to want to.

One movement may then cue another, like one word cues the next. What you do is surrender to the current of movement as it grows and changes. You keep checking in with the sensation, and move with its tide. It's a call and response.

Now let the movement get bigger—more of whatever it is. Say the word "intensify" to yourself. Alternate between perceiving more finely and urging it to grow. Keeping your eyes closed, pay attention inside. Magnify whatever is happening. A whisper may be more whispery, a shake more shaky. Accept the invitation. The more you give yourself to this movement, the deeper your shift will be. We are about shift here, that's the purpose, so don't stint or be stingy. Put your fullness into it.

movement turns to feeling and feeling turns to movement

You might notice an evolution of movement, but you do not direct. You observe it, and respond. That's all you need to do.

After five minutes or so of letting it get bigger and stronger, bring your attention to your mouth. Does a sound make a shape from the mindstate that you're in? Feel the lips and the tongue, and let a sound float on out. It may be a gurgle or a shuffle or a cackle or a squeak.

As the mouth shape and sensation start to acquire a quality, imagine a letter of the alphabet that makes that sound. And then, gradually, directly, eyes half-open enough to find the pen and paper, you start with the first letter, and the letter starts a word. It may be a nonsense word, but you keep moving from that. Now write the next word, then write the next. It may turn to English, you have no idea. The writing does it by itself, that's why it's automatic; your conscious mind only supplies the instruction, "Keep moving the pen."

THE MIND OF IT (THINKY THOUGHTS):

Have you ever watched a baby? Does it worry about whether it looks strange waving its arms about crazily, letting its tongue gurgle out? Being aware of yourself as "seen," thinking about "looking like this or that," sure has its drawbacks. (Like the absence of freedom.) Adults rarely take the permission that the baby's movements suggest.

So why did the child stop following impulses? You were a child, so you would know. Maybe someone laughed at the child in school and called him a dork. Chastened, the child decided that real spontaneous physical expression was a mistake, for the rest of his life. Unless you're "mentally ill," you have no permission. The body solidifies and limits. Business is good in the chiropractic trade.

So what did we do in this interior terrarium? We allowed the body itself to express its imagination. Usually that's only allowed in the "inside" of the mind.

You might just want to take a second, before we leave this section of work, to think about an *embodied* imagination. What would that mean? How does gesture move to trance? What would it be like if the body echoed the movement of dreams? In dreams you don't have a logical reason why Peter suddenly shows up and then turns into a goat. In dreams, things change that way on their own. You can analyze or interpret the dream, but it did it by itself. What would the body move like, then, if it changed that way too? And what writing would emerge from the pen in the wake of that tow?

Re-visions: Working on Your Piece from the Improvisational Mind

(In Which Our Hero Works on Her Piece Without the Critiquing)

So you may say, "OK, sure, right, you can draft and sketch from The Subconscious, but when it comes to crafting and polishing this writing, to making a Well-Oiled Machine, it's very straightforward. And it's *hard*. We've got to make it acceptable to the Committee of Judgement that sitteth on high and discriminates the Good from the Bad." (This is known as the "It's OK for kids to play, but adulthood has serious responsibilities" theory.)

And I may reply, "Well, I've got a Master's Degree in Revision, and I say it's still a playground, unless you wanna make it into a dungeon."[1] Why are we so committed to being stuck about this revising thing? It's because we've thought the only way to do it is to riddle ourselves with recriminations. "No no no no *no,* you dummy! Not that. *This!*" Or "I thought it was working and great but now I am in a *bad mood* and all of it is *crap!*" The delighted child withers.

So (you say), "Are you actually going to try to make a case for revising in the sublime?"

---

[1] And here in San Francisco, dungeons are playgrounds!

And then I say, "That's right. I am."

no need to beat the puppy
—Jack Kornfield

First off: Let's see revision as a kind of Vision. It's a re-Vision. A blindfolded-and-spun-around-and-given-smelling-salts-and-Wow!-now-I-see-it reVision. Like a mystical vision. Revising allows you to co-conjure with your words that came before. You felt something, and wrote it. And now you check those words and phrases against your original feeling. Are they in sync with what you were *nnnnngghh*ing to say?

And sometimes, it doesn't *quite* fit.[2] You say to yourself, "What this piece doesn't yet say is _____." And so you write that down. You try to describe this world we live in, or your internal world, and the language pushes back, the reality of the world pushes back. The lack of fit is a gift: we teach ourselves things by writing.

And here's some reassurance: There *is* a someone out there, helping you write. You are talking to that someone. This person is your own self. Your future self. Revision is a collaboration with self over time.

Revision is a collaboration with self over time.

And this person is helping you, which means you can trust yourself in freewriting. You know that you can come back later and look at that experimental phrase you scrawled madly. When you are freewriting, you put in "aardvark" and "vermiculite" and kept streaming forward. Your goode and pleasant compadre, The Later You will come back to it, and, with her mind that is by-definition different, she will determine if "aardvarks shoveling vermiculite" was really the way you wanted to say it. Or not. She will be happy to have The Past-Time You there to help her with a wildly-written inspiration of unbridled wacko-osity to choose

2 This is actually a good thing.

from. Don't leave her with some lifeless leftovers of used-up cautious platitudes.

Lemme give you a hint of what we'll be playing with next. The first trick of revision is to start with addition. Feel a sense of plenty by writing a

Platypuses, not platitudes.

lot. Plenty is good because it allows freedom in the future. For one, if you have to cut, you can cut from a place of abundance, instead of trying to dragoon one micro-filament of Good Writing at a time out of your tiny little text till you get enough . . . and that only barely. Starting with plenty allows you to avoid being miserly and having to patch bits and pieces together, scrimping up a hairpin here and a potato chip there.

But even more, plenty allows you to come back and see where the energy rises in your piece, where it has charisma and muscle. And when you see that charisma, you can let the other parts, the not-so-luminary parts, drop easily away. It's kind of like Taoism: you just let the water flow easily down the hill. You don't need that effortful fix-it mind.

And also, one more good thing. Revising also revises ourselves, because we teach ourselves things through our writing: You discover your own life by adding to and changing and working a freewrite, shifting it, aligning it more and more with what you feel to be true. Because by writing, you have revised your own mind.

PERSPECTIVE ON EVERYTHING NUMBER THIRTY-ONE

Mess-Makings and Energy Risings

(In Which our Hero Praises Disorder and Discovers the Center of Gravity)

First, let us take this opportunity—gathered here today—to extol mess! Tidiness had its clock cleaned by the Jazz Age, then gained ground in the McCarthy fifties, but the chaotic, paisley hairdos came back to us in a glorious beaded Summer of Mess. (Ever wonder why they didn't call it "The summer of clear, well-marked transitions and logical cohesion of suppository-shaped sentences"?) Let us beware that we Do Not Get Fooled Again.

You see, because in the world of nature, puma pouncings and bamboo forests and peregrine falcons emerged from chaos, which the science people tell us is not "chaos" but patterns more complex than we can initially discern. Turbulence has created all the excellent things of the world: the soil that grew your food, mambo and samba, the coastline of Norway, this excellent book. So please do not apologize for mess.

TRY IT!

Let us start with looking at the anti-model. Here is the old model for How to Write: Start with an outline. ("All good writing starts with an outline.") The introduction will be a shiny, ratchet-in-socket overture, and then we march orderly-like on to the parade grounds to the Body of the Essay, where cause will precede effect, and problem will be followed by solution. The Compare-and-Contrast battalions will be symmetrical to the last detail. All speculation (if allowed at all) will be solidly hedged. No crumpled-up sheets of paper. No dangling modifiers or anything else. No dried crusty bits, no slimy oozy bits, no prickly icky bits. Hup, two, three, four.

The virtue of this model is that it prevents anything sleazy from coming out. Thank god! Also it's efficient like the office. Aerodynamic. Worker productivity rises. More blood per ounce of stone. The ticker tape chugs out an ever higher profitability index. The 2 p.m. mind has triumphed! No more night sweats or inadvertent moans. No gargoyles; no clove cigarette smoke through the venetian blinds. The report is printed up on 20 lb. paper and filed away in the proper, space-saving, ergonomically designed brushed-steel office.

But what happens when, just by chance, and through no fault of your own, your writing is not like that?

The office staff gets huffy. Someone calls security. (Security gets called when there is insecurity.) "Don't tell us about tangled sheets and torrid nights. Don't tell us about menstrual blood. Don't talk about the little boys pouring salt on the slug. It doesn't fit into our idea! Get that disorder out of here."

So there you are on the cold pavement of the financial district, punted out the door by the security guard, clutching your manuscript. What now?

You make friends with Mess.

Mess has the characteristics of trains of derailed thought, abrupt shifts of tone, discontinuous and incommensurate freewrites in bumpy proximity, and scratched out half-starts. But mess also has the characteristic of having one or more *centers of gravity*. It has tendencies, outcroppings. Mess has a place where the energy rises. And that's what we're looking for. Energy. In mess, things arise and subside.

The complexity and intrigue of mess in writing is often beyond the antennae of the immediate mess maker, the freewriting You. But, because "revision is a collaboration with self over time," you don't worry about the complexity and structures and potentials while mess making, because the helper bee of your later self *will* come back around, tune into the power spots, agglomerate them together, re-sequence and make something, Pow! that you can show to your parents and best friend and all those naysayers who never knew anything anyway.

So, for this—the tangled-kelp model of revising—the first step is what you have already been doing in all these different barnstorming experiments. You let what comes to pass come to pass, (and that *does* take more time than the efficiency model, be ye forewarned). Let your writing be beyond what you can understand. That is how it will be great. But don't worry about "great." Worry about mess. Or, more properly, don't worry about mess.

What you've been doing all through this book here is kicking up a lot of dust, leaving all kinds of spurs, burrs, and flaky fragments everywhere. (In fact—sneaky me to not tell you this all along—a whole heap of these stunts I've been turning you on to are already re-Visions.)

So go get a freewrite or essay or mess that you've been making, and walk up next to it, curious and open, and try to see where the energy does rise. The first step in loving its mess and using that mess for your own purposes will be going through and marking those places—without negation of any kind—where electricity sings. (Friends are also good for this purpose because they can see energy through the clatter and whir of the half-started parleys, through all the mixed recycling of punctuation, and through the scattered soil amendments of thoughts and theories. Ask them simply, "Where do you feel the centers of gravity are in this piece? But please don't tell me anything else.")[3]

But you can do this by yourself. You look over the piece and try to notice the quickening of the voice, the souped-up language, the engagement and excitement. With your green pen in hand (green for go), you page through your mess, your lovely mess, and circle the energy risings. (Energy rises usually when you are writing what you want to write, and not what you've told yourself that you must write.)

satisfy yourself first,
then reader cannot fail to receive telepathic shock
and meaning-excitement by same laws
operating in his own human mind.
—Jack Kerouac

Warning: If you are judgement-focussed when you come back to look at the writing, the Energy Risings technique is harder to pull off. You will focus on what you don't like. You will get yourself

[3] See Chapter 10 for ways to get the use of other people's eyes without the dangers of their derailings. . .

Bummed Out. Instead, let curiosity peek around, like a child looking for sightings of what children are always looking for: Wonder.

Now, if you plan to show this piece of writing eventually to
others, you know that later when you are combing and preening,
you will be focusing on gentleness, smoothness, and generosity,
but now you focus on the Energy. Remember that the universe
started in a flash of light, and has evolved itself into this vast
seafood gumbo by simply following its own pleasures. This,
however, took time. For this technique, it is good to have time.

Do nothing and all things will be done.
Let the water flow naturally downhill.

Then, as you let things re-constellate like little metal filings
shimmying around magnetic poles, you can let other things drop
away. That "dropping away" might mean cuts or subtractions, or
just a shift in emphasis next time you add to the piece, and the
"re-constellating" might mean a playful resequencing and group-
ing of those bits that sing—the places you have circled. We'll talk
about that more as we go on. Either way, with that mimosa taste
in your mouth, you will blissfully let go of the less-than-best. It
is because you feel the distance between the sumptuous-and-
right, and the pallid or clunky, because you are so lusciously
swanked by the sumptuous as you ride the snazzy taxi of your
delight, the less-than-luminary flutters out between your fingers
without your second thought. Yes, Dearie, that is where you let it
go. Let it go because you love energy. Let it go because sweetness
and juice are your mantras. Let it go. Let it go. Let it go.

Once you've lost the parts you realize you don't even really
like that much, you can follow the electricity vibrations and the
rice pudding sensations. Then the gists start to congregate with
each other through the Goddess of Re-Sequencing, the glitches
repattern themselves into a smooth little humming perpetual
motion machine, and your piece of writing becomes a gyroscope
powering an endless etch-a-sketch in the golden fields of the lord.

STORM THE BASTILLE NUMBER THIRTY-TWO
Break the Art Museum Rule

(In Which Our Hero Finally Says What She Means, and Re-envisions by Means of Addition)

Here's the beleaguered writer: "The problem with this piece of writing is that . . . nnnnngghhh! I'm so *frustrated*."

Here are some varieties of this: "I want to tell about abandoning atheism without sounding hokey and I don't know how to do it." Or "Does the monkey die in the end?" Or "I can't fix the part about the brother because I can't decide if he's gonna break up with the pimp or not." Or "If I reveal that much about Sarah, people are going to think it's about me (which it partly is, but in some ways not), and I don't want to have to write, 'it's only me in *some* parts and not in the others, so please don't think that I did *that*.'" Or "I'm trying to get the piece to feel like my experience of being guided even though I didn't know I was being guided." All these are varieties of "nnnnngghhh."

So you are thinking all these things *about* what you are writing, but someone inside is telling you, "You can't actually *write* those questions about the writing down in the report/novel/poem!"

Hey, that's just like in the art museum! On the little plaque next to the painting, you can write "acrylic on canvas" but not "my mommy died." And maybe you can write some blather like, "The artist is expressing the fundamental rupture between Knowing and Being in a highly-mediated environment." But you absolutely cannot, will not, do not write, "The threads that are torn across the piece of chicken wire represent how I think my boyfriend is a jerk, and the little spatterings of red paint represent my desire to merge with the universe that's been stymied by the outsourcing of holiness to India." That's called *explaining* the artwork, and the first thing you learn in art school is, "That is *so* wrong." After several years in classes, you refine this statement to, "Well, if you can't *get* it by looking at it, maybe there's nothing *for you* to get." All of this is as if the whole purpose of making and looking at art was a way to admit only certain people to a tenth-grade clique of popular girls and keep out everybody else.

Well, for this piece, I'm going to suggest that you be open to just saying what you feel *about* the writing *in* the writing. Or to the questions you have about this piece. Or to what you are trying to accomplish, and putting that down on the page. Or to why you are frustrated with it, or how you don't know which way to go. Why not?

"Because art is a highly-mediated symbol structure in which implicit demands on the reader's attention are mediated by the communicative imperative, which simultaneously underscores the . . ."

Exclusion seems to be their purpose.

Now, having stated my point in way-too-extreme a manner, let me modulate it slightly. Perhaps you are saying to yourself, "Well, if I *know* that *The Journal of Anthroposophical Diatonic Humility* only accepts papers in a certain prescribed form, what's the point of screeding all over the page about what nimbuses they are, and how I feel my brain is a factory reject, and the real point of my article is the holiness anyway? They won't accept a paper with all that stuff in it, so if I write it down, I'll only take it out later because I *know* that they won't accept it. It makes no sense to put something in to take it right out."

Well . . . Breaking The Art Museum Rule is about saying "Yes." Saying "yes" to impulses. Impulses originate in the owl-filled night. When we say "No" to an impulse, the flow stops. Boom. Game over. Then we get all jammed up like ohms of resistance in a copper wire.

We here at The Church of Re-Visions and Renditions believe in the transformatory power of going for it. In keep the pen moving. Let the electrons flow and all will be taken care of. Remember *you can take it out if you don't like it later.* It's important to let the keystrokes fall where they may.

TRY IT!

Try explaining. Try "tell don't show." Explain your problem. Scribble down your dream for what this piece might be. Bombast your way through the question marks.

For example: "I'm trying to make revision sound and feel as intriguing and interesting as I know it can be, and have experienced it as being, without having the readers fight me too much, and still have it fit their experience." Or try writing, "My editor Lynette is going to read this manuscript before any of the other readers and if I keep in that line about 'getting away with it' at the end of this section, she'll be hip to my game, and the whole house of cards is going to fall down." *Say* that. Write it. Don't sit there neurotically *thinking* about "the problem" forever and ever like you were going to live to three hundred. Unload it. Dump it on the page and move forward. Because you don't know what's *behind* those thoughts. What's behind is what's interesting. Trust me.

And once the little troll who's blocking your path to finishing your essay on Shakespeare gets his jollies by spewing out all the questions and contingencies and little doubts he's all fixated on, then the essay can come out easily because the troll lets you pass over the bridge. And sometimes—this is an unexpected bonus, and you often don't discover this until revision six—that while the troll was cross-examining your writing, he uttered one little word, which you didn't even notice at the time, but that has miraculously turned out to be *just the word* that the whole bloomin' Shakespeare paper hinges on! It's the fulcrum, by George, the pivot, and the troll just picked it out of his rabbit-crowded top hat.

So *do* break the art museum rule, and put "The reason I'm doing this is ____" down there, right in the midst of the document. Or write, "Should Simon chuck the gun out the window or not?" Or admit (there on the page), "I'm wanting something more, something different, and that is _____ ." Or ask—in ink, not in your head—"What words can I use to make atheism sound just too old hat without seeming like the kind of person that I don't want to seem like?"

Try putting it out there—whatever you're not allowed to say. And try it more than once. It may take some again and again (which can also be cool). Who knows, it might even be possible, as you and I together create a better world than the one we live in today that *all that stuff can stay in the final piece exactly as is.* You've read this book all this way, and just *see* how much I've gotten away with. *The Journal of Anthroposophical Diatonic Humility* will never be the same.

THE MIND OF IT:

Remember, the universe has a lot of things going on that we don't know about. We have no *idea* what the universe is like. What it wants to have happen. We don't know what's trying to come through us. Maybe the unburdening, the steam bursting out of the pressure cooker whistle of the article intended for *The Journal of Anthroposophical Diatonic Humility* has another destination. Maybe *we* have another destination. Say Yes to what is trying to come through you and *Shazam!* you're answering a score of seemingly unrelated problems that seem to be about this piece of writing, but—you find out years later—are answers to other pieces of writing, or to issues in your life, or to problems you were going to have in the future but now won't because you broke The Art Museum Rule.

INCREDIBLE LEVERAGE DEVICE THAT YOU
NEVER KNEW NUMBER THIRTY-THREE

The Great Gateway
of Dissonance[4]

(In Which Our Hero Starts Sleuthing for Potency
in the Tangled Clottings of Syntax)

So here's our question, Andy: When are you going to get serious about *real* revising? We don't believe all this hippie fluff
about letting it Happen. Everyone knows, and you can't hide it,
that revising is about finding the awkward parts and making
them better. It's about correcting the youthful excesses of the
improvisatory mind and getting down to brass tacks! It's about
making all parts of the elegiac poem as elegiac as the best parts.
Stop beating around the truism!

OK, OK: let's play with that one, then.

So there you are humming along, doing your real revising
with your unfinished tune and all of a sudden, "bleep!" the note
sounds off. There is discord in the Family of Man. You use the
word "pelican" when you meant to write "Peloponnesian." So you
fix-it-change-it. Or the piece is moving too slow when you think
it should move fast. So you fix-it-change-that. Trim a little bit over
here and a lotta bit over there. Wrong mood. Incongruous example. Oops, I forgot to explain that Sheila is Sam's sister.

This search, this grand search, is a search for *dissonance*.
Dissonance. The unexpected, the "that which does not fit." The
jarring, the quirky, the confounding, the "error": writing is full of
sharp jabby objects that don't fit harmonious-istically with one of
thousands of mental maps. Writing is rife with spelling and usage
mistakes—you forgot and put "do" and "are" next to each other,
as in, "People do are great." Writing is clotted with dundancies

[4] Thanks and gratitude to Bill Robinson of the English composition
program at San Francisco State for the first clue for this idea. And may he
forgive me . . .

and redundancies—all of a sudden you realize you've described the old man's voice as "warm and intimate" seven separate, important-sounding times. Writing can even be wrong (!). The spell check didn't catch the difference between "loose" and "lose," and you read over your pages and find to your horror that your protagonist wasn't feeling *looser* after a few drinks but *loser*. You are stricken, and you are striking the page with angry red gashes. "Dissonance!" you cry. Cut it out! And that's why revising sucks, right? Because it's like spending eight hours treating wounds in the burn ward. Well, OK, I agree, fix and polish can be miserable. But it's also sometimes like spit and polish. I mean you *could* be the little boy putting the final touches of paint on the scale model of a balsa-wood bi-plane. Yessss! Just right!

Hmmm. So *sometimes* revising is misery, and other times it isn't. Maybe revising is all drat and darn when we have dyspepsia, and all glimmering and tropical-vacation when we're doused in benediction. That is to say, maybe it's mood dependent. Or maybe revising is good when we're puffed up and proud that we've pulled out a plum and what a good boy am I, and it's all slimy with ooze when the world has turned up its snout at our precious baby, or we *think* that world will turn up its snout, or when we are indulging ourselves in some nightmare that the world would love *nothing better* than to go out of its way to show us that it is turning up its snout at our writing, or when the world doesn't even bring its snout anywhere *near* our precious baby because it's too busy downloading porn or text messaging some other snout on the subway. And *that's* when revision sucks.

Well, all that's true in its own complex and irresolvable way, but the best advice for all that is *generosity*. Just give. A giving of—dare I say it?—niceness. Go through your work and smooth out its mean and selfish edges. Don't be mean to yourself, just think about delighting a single sweet reader that you care about. They are trying to learn what you know about Patagonia and you don't want them to fumble over a lot of "of which is what the thing to be at the place where it was . . ."

How-*ever!*

There's one secret trick and you are gonna be happy that you know it. It's pleasing! Here it goes. (I'm starting with an example.)

Say, let's just say, that you are really good at spelunking. You even like the *word* "spelunking." You can amble over stalagmites. You can wiggle through crannies in a wetsuit with a halogen light on your forehead. You are discursive at cocktail parties about limestone deposits or the great unsolved mystery of the Ailwee caves of Ireland. Now let's also say that you spent far too much of your adolescence reading *The Hobbit* and *The Lord of the Rings*, over and over again. You can recite the entire dynasties of the Kings of Numenor. You've read all the redacted texts, have a life-long membership in the Society of Tolkein Scholarship and you're current on the flaming battles over whether Orcish is a sneering form of Cockney and indicates the intolerable class bias of an effete Oxford don.

Now let's add just one more in there. Say you are *also* proficient at, no in fact really, really top of the line at, paper-scissors-rock.

Now let's take this hypothetical situation into a practical application. You are spelunking with your fellow spelunkologists. Sitting down for a break after an arduous bit of cranny-squeezing, you start playing a good spate of paper-scissors-rock. You're winning nine out of ten hands. Nobody knew you were that good. But you're used to their shock: you put yourself through college winning money, big money, at paper-scissors-rock. Their awe is all too familiar to you. "How can someone win every single time like that at paper-scissors-rock?" etc. etc. etc. You've heard it all before.

But this time, something different happens. One of the people with you decides to start quizzing you on exactly who came between Arathorn of the Dunedain and his grandson Arador. And that's when it happens. That's when you blow it. You start losing at paper-scissors-rock! Cognitive overload . . . and dissonance creeps in. Game after game you lose, and the orcs take the beach.

And that's what happens every so often during writing. You are re-reading your work, and you come upon a sentence that is syntactically frazzled, not elegiac like you want. And as much as I know that you feel the bitter bite of wormwood in your mouth, finding it, I'll stand here today and tell you that this discovered dissonance is in fact a good thing, a time to be glad and rejoice.

TRY IT!

Gus Bagakis is working on a book. It's called *What Is a Class Analysis and Why Do We Need One?* In his draft copy, he comes upon the following sentence:

> The goal of those aware of the alienation, hopelessness, economic inequity, etc. of a society with class divisions is to overcome class, to create a society where all people are equally valuable and respected, rendering the focus on the mental/manual split irrelevant.

So many nice parts. But there's just a little bit of hard-to-read in there. A thing we might call dissonance. Old-school writing advice goes like this (All hail Strunk and White!): "You must get in there and fix this thing. The problem here, for one, is that the noun 'goal' is overly separated from the predication 'is to overcome class,' so you should re-write the sentence and get them closer together. Now point two about this sentence is that you have a weak verb. It says right here to avoid 'be' verbs. Can't you make this an active verb? Lastly, you've got a lot of prepositional phrases in here, 'of those aware,' 'of the alienation,' 'of a society,' 'with class divisions,' 'on the split,' and so on. So we need to use other kinds of sentence doohickeys in there to tighten this sentence up."

So . . . you know what: all of that is *true*. And if Gus goes in there and ethnically cleanses all the barbs and jabs and stumbles out of his sentence, it will be better. But. When we do that we miss a clue. A very important clue. Because when Gus was crafting that sentence, most likely, he was in a situation in which he was in cognitive overload. He was thinking about a lot of ideas—

the goal of people being equally valued, about the mental/manual split, about hopelessness and inequality and alienation—and he was also thinking about them *all at the same time*. And also trying to write a sentence. And those ideas were important to him and important to the World. But because he was juggling important ideas, *and* all the emotions attached to big problems like class society and alienation, syntax got a little tangled.

So here's the point: you don't want to go through and just *eliminate* all the parts that are the very markers and clues from you, for you, that something important was being written about, the word-order fumbles that indicate you were handling something really important to you, that show you that you are reaching for something deeper or more complex. You may be in a bit over your head. But that's good. That's where you can delve. That's where your writing will grow. That's where your writing can *cause you* to grow.

So instead of rushing to just *fix* that "problem," what you do is you circle that little stumbly sentence and you copy it out, all of it, at the top of a new page. Now you launch into a freewrite that can show you what you were reaching to say. You use those same words, but you don't just rewrite the sentence; you keep going into all the parts of it that lie underneath it, the parts not said, or almost said. Keep pushing against "What I was trying to say here was _____ ." And "What I mean by this is _____ ." Maybe write for five full minutes on just this one point and see where you get to. Especially watch what happens near the end of the freewrite. Keep pushing against what was trying to be said.

THE MIND OF IT:

Dissonant phraseology tells you about your mind at the moment of conception; it's a marker, a gateway, to something you are trying to know. The red "Awk!" ink is the *last* thing you need. That is like when the rationalist says that it's not that moonlight in mist is transporting, it's that the ocular retina is undergoing a stress reaction to the perceptual cortex and thus the sense of everyday reality we are used to is altered by a decrease in the verifiability of the sensory data perceived. So don't let that happen. Do not smudge out the doorway to the arcane with a bossy little formula about the prepositional phrase.

RELIEF FROM THE TYRANNY OF MINIMALISM NUMBER THIRTY-FOUR

Micro-Detailing and Sensory Infusion

(In Which Our Hero Puts Accretions of Sensation in Her Text and Feels the Soothing Aspects of Plenty)

Thin. Writing can be thin. Just for an example of "thin," take a look at the kind of writing in a contract. Holy Cannoli! What empty! All those words and not a single drop of juice!

The user agrees to make no claim for any reason whatsoever against the corporation, its members or agents or employees or owners of the premises for loss, theft, damage or destruction or for any injury to . . .

Thin!

Where are the singed pineapples? The sordid beachcombers? The beer-bums in flip-flops? What's wanted is an infusion of details: add them on like a swarm of seabirds darkening the sky. Addition is a form of revision, and let us praise its name. Let us have an affluence of copious extravagance:

The user agrees to make no claim for any reason whatsoever against the corporation, its members, or parts of their bodies or bad habits or agents and their home mortgage insurance or their lemon meringue pie recipes or employees or their grievances against their

jerk bosses or shuddering illuminations in the middle of the night or
owners of the premises *or owners of useless junk that neighbors sell
each other at yard sales,* or the disingenuous tricksters that spirit
away some porcelain doohickey from an old lady for 25 cents and
then sell it as a "collectable" on eBay for $4,500 or *for loss, or grief
or heartache* or theft or damage or destruction *or failing grades or
bad-tasting soup or candy apples* or for *any injury to tantalizing little
pieces of knowledge lost in a cave in Tibet in the early second century
or to translations of Dostoyevsky published in Hindi or . . .*

What we want is a whole Hawaii of details slathered in every
crease and crevice of your already-existing text. A regular hagiog-
raphy celebrating a coruscation of abundance, an oyster shell
mound of extra!

TRY IT!

1. Take 2/3 cup of already-written writing.

2. Fold in butter and sugar in appropriate proportions (for a
creamier broth, use in inappropriate proportions).

3. Add in bits and pieces of the tiniest size.

4. Whip egg yolks into a frenzy and carefully slop over the
edges of the bowl.

5. Drunkenly spill grated small words (hark, midge, welch,
imp, to, if and or but).

6. Drizzle with details uncalled for (". . . which reminds me of
how Aunt Marge always used to have to go out to the chicken
shack at 3 A.M. with little Ralph's high-powered squirt gun full of
lemon juice to squirt into the eyes of the raccoons trying to kill
themselves more chickens. It was quite a sight, Marge in her
nightshirt, chicken feathers flying, the raccoons clinging to the
chicken wire and baring their teeth, the chickens screeching up
the air, two large male raccoons above Marge's head, Marge in full
Scarface mode protecting tomorrow's breakfast omelette with high
powered blasts of concentrated lemon juice from the super soaker,
and Marge shouting Kyaa!! Kyaa!! Kyaa!!, well, I tell you . . .").

7. Daub with sensory words of sight, sound, and smell:

balcony ⇨ corrugated balcony;

battery acid ⇨ stone-faced battery acid;

schnoz ⇨ bloated, disgusting schnoz;

concept ⇨ tremulous concept;

guitar solo ⇨ brand name guitar solo corrupted by years of too many Charlie Parker records and long distance truck rides with insane hitchhikers telling stories of spiritual awakenings encrusted with incorrect references to arcane Norse legend

8. Let rise!

OK! Start writing! Kyaa![5]

THE MIND OF IT:

Yes, yes I know, the oldest trick in the How to Write book: "Concrete, specific details, blah, blah, blah." And, furthermore, let's not forget those annoying kinds of novels that are just *larded* with every dust crack and shoulder shrug and dependent clause and footnote that some speed junkie could think up. Let's all just agree right now that such things are Bad. And get over it. We're on the same page. And move on.

It is true, however, that so often we yearn for plenty, and do not know that is what we are yearning for. We suffer in Lacksville while the tide of abundance roars by our ears—with us hearing nothing. We forget about addition.

[5] Possible Objection:

"Hey, but waita minute, Mr. A! What if we don't want all of your crazy hallucinations in our prize-winning short story? What if that feels like an overdone mescaline saucepan? We want an incredibly dense piece of language poetry that ratchets the reader to the floor with the brilliance of our perfect sharp imagery!"

Well, I anticipated that objection (in fact I wrote it). And here's the answer: you don't have to *keep* all that stuff. You just add it in to give yourself the wonderful German Chocolate Cake sense of plenty. You can minus it later. The enemy here, as I said before, is thin.

Also, the subconscious *likes* plenty. When you finally get through to the subconscious that you really are going to give it free reign, it blossoms, like plankton in the Pacific. And then, when the subconscious is rolling, high rolling, you get stuff: nuggets, insights, turns of phrase, the tone you've been looking for. Yes, you might have to go back through and take some stuff out later, but you will end up with more livid writing (vivid? sure, that too). Writing with more pith and punch. And you do want your writing to kick ass, don't you? Admit it!

And don't get me wrong, I love minimalism (though you'd hardly know it from *this* pandemic!), but even minimalism needs juice, just like everything else. It needs juice and wasabi, and chili and brie.

UNEXPLAINABLE MYSTERY NUMBER THIRTY-FIVE
Tuning Fork

Have you ever written something that you are *very* happy with? Even one paragraph? One that you can look at and say, "Yes, this is me, and I like it?" I hope so. And you've probably wished that you could write "like that" more of the time. That's what this technique allows you to do. Tuning Fork will help you get inside another mind, and that other mind will be the mind that wrote that passage before. A sublime mind.

All you need for this is a little stretch of your own work that feels good to you. In which you recognize yourself. This scraplet of your writing is your ticket that can trigger a re-Vision of some other piece of yours that is resisting you.[6]

Here's how it works. You take this old piece, and you tune your mind to the same resonating frequency as the mind that wrote it, the You long ago. Simple, isn't it? The mind that wrote it is still in residence in the background geiger-count of the words.

---

[6] Gratitude to Richard Seyd (www.seydways.com), inventor of The Trigger Approach (used in the theater) which gave me the start of this idea.

You re-enter the state of mind through its visible products: the words themselves, their patterns, and the spaces between them. (You can also do Tuning Fork with another person's work, and that can be really mystical, too.)

The way to do this is in steps, increments. For writing emerges, all writing emerges—this is a big one—from that tiny instant of moving forward, in that feeling impelled to say "the next thing," and to say it in a way that matches the exact feeling inside. That impulse to move forward is not just any old impulse, but a constellation of sensations of a certain flavor and type. It's a follow-the-leader kind of game, but "leader" in the sense used by botanists and arborists, "the shoot, the bud, which grows at the apex of the stem." And that's the re-Vision we are looking at here, a re-writing from a precise place of mind, that is cued, triggered, from that leaf-bud, wing-tip, stretch-out-into-new-space impulse. And we use the patterns of language itself to finely tune the ever-shifting, pliable mind.

TRY IT!

The first thing to do is to set in front of your mind what you are writing about or revising or rewriting—that essay, story, or poem. Perhaps you are stuck about that place in the story where the boat is coming to the shore with the seminarian, and you don't want to be too obvious about the *idea* that you are trying to get across, and at the same time, when your friend read your piece she said she didn't understand what you were trying to say. You have to say *something* there, but every time you've tried to write it, it comes out clunky or weird or unsavory for one reason or another. You want to get into the right mindspace to write it in the way that you have envisioned.

So once you have a piece you want to work on, the next step is to take out your little shred of gold from before, those one or two paragraphs that illuminate your world. Your criterion for choosing this piece is that it possesses that "just so" feeling that says, "This sounds like me."

Now you don't wanna *analyze* it, but that shred-of-gold writing has in it certain choices of words, and a particular way that spaces appear between them, and a rhythm they create in the mind that reads it. All these aspects are an afterimage of the mind that wrote that piece of writing, and thus the piece is a doorway back into it. To step back into that mind, you want to re-enter the impulse that moves the pen and mind forward. There's a propulsion to this impulse: it may be a jet propulsion impulse, or a tiny mincing footstep impulse, but it carries you forward in a particular way.

the impulse to write is an impulse to move forward

The trick here is to create a mindstate similar enough to the original one that the impelling moves forward on its own, without guessing or figuring. This is done by recreating a physical pattern in the mind's ear. And that's where the tuning fork comes in. [7]

So what we'll be doing is taking that story or that letter to the congressman or that song lyric or that Mission Statement for the Organization, or whatever it is that you feel stuck about, and use Tuning Fork to get to a place to re-write it. But please remember: this is not about fixing something broken, but finding a way to re-envision it from the place of mind that you love. Let me also just say that this takes a few minutes of prep and energy at the outset. It's worth it, but you know that it takes putting energy in.

So you've got the piece you want to work on, the golden passage to re-see, and do you still have some index cards? Scraps of paper would work too. Then we can start.

Take the piece-of-gold writing and put it in front of you now. What you will do is . . . to break it . . . into parts. Take each phrase, sub-phrase, the smallest meaningful bit, of two words, or four, and put that on one of your index cards.

---

[7] This is in the re-Vision section, so it's part of the re-seeing bag of tricks. But you can use it for a fresh piece of writing too.

Here's a "fer instance" piece of writing. It was written by my friend Adam Kinsey. You would use your own, but just to show, here it is:

> Sitting on the steps of the church, he
> watched the dogs carve the twilight,
> spin on each other and roll in the park
> across the street. His chest felt like
> it was crammed full of flowers, slowly
> rotting.

You take the pieces:

> Sitting on the steps
> of the church,
> he watched the dogs
> carve the twilight
> spin on each other
> and roll
> in the park . . . (etc.)

and put one on each card. You might want a piece of writing a bit longer than this for yourself, but that'll do for this examply-type-a thing.

Now what about the tuning part? Here's how it works:

You stack up the cards, in order, and you read the first one out loud. Into the air! And then, *without looking at the next card*, you speak out the next phrase, as close as you can get. *Caution:* This is *not* about memorizing something. Don't memorize, or think that you should try to. Also: Tuning Fork is not a guessing game or about getting it right for the exam. All those approaches will cause you to clench, and you don't want clenching. You want to sense and feel the rhythm and flavor. Just read the first card and without looking say out loud what's on the second, as best as you can.

Then look at the second card and notice the difference.

Now, the interesting part. Reflect for just a second on why you thought it was "at the church" with your right-now mind, when it was actually "of the church." Please don't analyze. *Please* don't berate yourself. Just reflect for a second, and go back again to card one, read it aloud, then read card two aloud and say into the air (without looking) what you think is on card three. You've got some idea because you just put this together, but hopefully you haven't memorized it. (If you memorize the piece, Tuning Fork doesn't work as well.) The part you *want* is the discrepancy, and the tiny moment to reflect, "Huh. That's interesting. Why did my right-now mind say 'watching the dogs' when my last-week mind said, 'he watched the dogs'?"

Keep going. That's the important part. It usually doesn't kick in for at least five or six phrases. You are not keeping score, you are just establishing a resonating frequency for your language-making brain. That's all. Keep going.

Get to the end, or to a place where you know, "I feel it," and go directly to the page. Write on your originally chosen topic or story or lyric or letter for ten minutes, or fifteen, and write freely, no stopping, whatever way naturally comes out.

QUESTIONS FOR THE CURIOUS:

This one's almost too mysterious to touch with analyzing-ology. So let's just feel what happened. Read it over and feel it.

THE MIND OF IT:

I think the biggest teaching I've gotten from this is how fabulously wise and *smart* the subconscious mind can be when we let it go. If you wanted to indulge your sense of wonder, you could compare the rhythms and the internal rhyme sequences, and the tenor and timbre of the new words that came out: all of them in some kind of congruency with the seed piece. See how much complexity can be managed by the mysterious circuitry.

John Chung, an actor, dancer, and a collaborator of mine said of this work, "The places where you consistently get it 'wrong' are where you have the greatest subconscious resistance. Each mistake is a gift; that point is a pressure point, a place where the entire piece can reveal itself and crack open."

And one last Cool Thing: You can try Tuning Fork with Ginsberg, or Wordsworth, or Mary Queen of Scots, or Mae West. Tune your mindspace to their exquisite ambrosia, and see where it goes.

COMPLETELY DIFFERENT OTHER THING NUMBER THIRTY-SIX

Radical Subtract and the Creativity of Minus

Here's you: "It's so perfect, I can't lose a single word. I worked so *hard*!" (Actually this is *me*. But we'll ignore that, in our genteel sort of way, thank you.) Yes, yes, yes. Good parents do not shunt their children into the discard pile. Try taking a newborn kitten from a cat and you'll find that out. Also, we here at Writing Open the Mind are *glad* that you love your words. Words should not be hated. Glory, glory hallelujah. But also,[8] who wants to lose the creativity of minus? Not us. Since your mind is gargantuan, part of its pleasure is in the creativity of taking away. And anyway, what's the problem with a little minus?

TRY IT!

Take a page, maybe a printed page, with a number of words. For example, a typed, double-spaced page is about 250 words. Choose a half of that page to start with. That's about 125. Our goal is to minus, to radically minus, to cut out a third. In this

---

[8] "Hey Andy, always with these 'but also's.' What's up with that?" Answer: the world is "both and," and I'm trying to hew close to the truth that this world is full of Much.

case, that'll be down to 83.333 words. That is your goal. Cut cut cut, cut cut cut cut. Don't be fainthearted. Take it all out!

But first, before we start it, a coupla rules:

- Try to keep the meaning, as much as you can.
- You can have sentence fragments. Don't worry.
- You may change "dangling" to "dangle," to make it make sense after you have minused some words, but don't work the thing too much. The focus is on cut.
- If you absolute need to, add in a "the" or "to" or "at."
- Go through once, then go through again. There's always some little bit else that still can be scratched out.
- Decide on a word count. A firm word count. I said cut one third. Maybe you want to go more radical than that. And without fail stick to it.[9] This is the important part. If you kinda go, "Oh well, I got close; there's no more to cut," you will miss a Big Part of the bang that minus can give. It's only in the push against ("I *can't* cut any more!" "But you *must* cut some more!") that you can actually break through and see beyond What You Already Know.

One way to get the Hang of this muscle that you are trying to build, is to try radical minus first with something not yours. Or you can start in directly on your very own piece. Why don't you start?

QUESTIONS FOR THE CURIOUS:

This one's a good one, definitely, to take a pause, and to reflect on. (Have you tried the experimundo? Try it, you will like it.) Was it hard to cut, to cut-cut-cut? What voices of delight or resistance came up? Did you have the experience of not seeing a possible cut, but under the brutal rule of "get it down to X number of words," you had to go back again? Doing this with other folkses is always enlightening: you see where you coulda cut that

[9] Secret: you can put it back *in* later, so please don't freak out.

you didn't before. Were you—even once—amazed at how little you need?

THE MIND OF IT:

Let's imagine that you have only so many calories between lunch and dinner. And let's say that you've picked up a book to read for pleasure. To decode each single word takes 0.023 microcalories. (I am making up numbers. You should try it yourself.) You spend those calories running eye over text and transmigrating it—through the Miracle of Interpretation—into stuff of brain. Now, what you are hoping as you are reading is that each word, in cohabitation with other words, releases its own little bang of energy, making the little controller gnome in the back of your mind say, "Yes! Yes, I want to keep reading this excellent writing! Give me *more!*" But like all aerodynamic projectiles, in writing there is always drag. We shall define drag as all the words that static you down, that muddy the tire treads, that cotton-candy the wiper blades as you try to drive through. Too much drag and you put down the book.

So on the aerodynamic efficiency level, radical minus on the part of the writer helps you be more generous and sweet to Ye Olde Reader, and give them good reasons to keep reading to the end. But writing is beyond creating words like smooth projectiles. There is also great fun to be had in minus. There's the delight of the punchier sentence. Bang! (Feels good, doesn't it?) And also the great feeling of burden dropped. "Oh gad! I don't need that!" You roll your shoulders as you put the heavy backpack of bricks down at the campsite.

But *even if* you have no intention of turning your thesis into a tone poem, there's still a *lot* you can get out of this. Because now that you've got it down to bones, bones, barren bones, you are now free to . . . add! Put new things in, redecorate. Put little rococo touches! Cherubs! Curlicues! Little frilly designs or arabesque geometrical patternings, or feng shui mirrors. You can do this now because now you are free of the incredible drowning weight of The Way It Came Out the First Time. The freedom to make something really actually different. That freedom is good. That's what this book is all about. The goodness of free.

Like all of these techniques, this one helps us break the petrified patterns that riddle our minds. You may even get a little embarrassed about how many bricks you've put in your rucksack all of these years. But, as they say, "Forgiveness is giving up all hope of ever having a better past."

And lastly, Radical Subtract lets us notice again, in a different way, that writing is indeed made of words. It's good to actually see the words: too often we forget because we're always aching toward *meaning*, and words sometimes seem like just implements, or junk in the way. But when we skinny on down to just the few that we *need*, we cherish the rare. We notice the angle and loft, the break of the arc, the cusp of the wisp.

The Inter-Subconscious: Working with a Writing Group to Find Your Own Mystery

So you want to join a writing group or class, but there's this Issue: Other people are so damn *unpredictable*.

Of course, *you* are unpredictable, too, and you'll remember that this whole book is actually about getting yourself to be less predictable, less boxy, more jinxed. So one of our sources—an inimitable source—of the unplannable is the other critters in the room with you. And yes, it's true, other people can be put to use for plenty of purposes to benefit your writing—wise feedback, trenchant analysis, ideas to steal, encouragement, sweetness, etc.—but let us not forget their excellent function of introducing the impossible into your life. (Don't you just love impossible people?) And if you think it's selfish and narcissistic to want to be around other people for the explicit purpose of having them throwing a pineapple at you from the left field of their terrarium, remember that your purpose, by the Correlative Principle,[1] is to fly in out of your left field and insinuate the wacko and bozo into *their* lives.

[1] I made that up.

But also, other people will also do tweaky things, so tweaky you'd think it was done by a rutabaga. Or worse. And although I'd like to put this part off for a while—you know, hide it deep in the middle of this chapter—I have to state it right here: it is an absolute true and factual fact that many writers have stopped writing because someone else said something hurtful to them about their work. Often it was a number of people. "Maybe you aren't cut out for writing." "Will you get to the point already?" (Pointy people seem to like points.) "This whole middle section has to go." (And who would know better than *I* what should or shouldn't be in your piece?)

Now this book isn't going to stop meanness and cruelty in the world. (Would that it could!) I'm not that delusional. (Yet.) And most of the time (though not always) when people say bad stuff to you, they are trying to help. Person A is trying to "improve" Person B's writing. And the reason he or she does that is that they think critiquing is the only way to help. The best thing, however, for acquiring new chops at writing, and for developing new awarenesses about your writing, is to *continue writing*, week in and week out. Injuring people so that they hate writing does not improve anything.

If you are one of the few people who doesn't have scars from trying to express yourself and then having someone else swoop in and say something like, "This is totally disorganized!" then count your blessed stars. But most of us have had far too much experience with the Discipline and Punish ideology of education. It's as if the whole society just can't help itself. Kind of a nervous tic: "Fix it! Fix it!" (Warning, rant coming.) This ideology is so sure of itself, so bully-pulpitted that it cannot hear flickerings, emergences. It is so jack-booted that it marches on to the gleaming beacon of progress and to hell with the snail darters. This concept wants to mold your mind toward some Platonic ideal. It has its ideal of what "good writing" is burned into its mind, and fails to notice how idiosyncratic its own idea is of what's Right and what's Wrong. Its sensitivity is so crushed that it has become unavailable to the tropical continent of possibility shimmering just below the waves.

And it likes to say, "I'm sorry I have to be so Objective here, but this needs A Lot of Work."

Try telling this voice that there are other ways to relate to a piece of writing, that other modes of discovery and illumination are possible, and this voice will say, "If you want to write, you are just going to have to *learn to take the criticism*." As if the criticism was the purpose for writing. It says criticized writing is good writing.

Now, far be it from me to cast any aspersions on the S&M community (where punishment *is* pleasure), but most of what happens during this kind of haranguing of your piece of writing is contraction—emotional contraction, physical contraction.

Contraction is not good for the ability to be sensitive, and it is not good for the blooming of the subconscious. It is true that there are people who can survive and even thrive in that Wild West Bruiser kind of world—and more power to them—but it's kind of like the conquistadors: they figure that they have invented steel and nautical devices and sailing ships, and because of that, the continent is theirs. They cannot see the incredible sensitivity that has allowed jungle hunters to read and speak bird calls high in the canopies; they don't understand the language that the medicine keeper speaks to the plants; they don't see the potency of a people who can live without extinguishing the food supply of their great, great, great grandchildren. They see none of that and say, "Ah, heathens; we must civilize them."

So in order to avoid that maelstrom of other people's attitudes, what do most people do? Just realize that the writing life is fundamentally lonely, and huddle off in our garret fulminating at the critics in our minds as we angrily wash the dishes?

Well . . . actually, that would be a mistake too. We'd lose something great. Because the quite excellent thing about these other rutabagas is that they really can donate a lot to your mix.

For one thing, they have their energy that can jumble the bingo-ball tumbler of your brain. It could be a wily crackpot energy from out of the blue, or it could be a slow and precise energy, or a deep and warm energy, or sprightly, or eerie, or dorky, or cranky. We welcome them all. Into the mix! You look at them across the circle and they are flopping their hands around like hamsters at a rave. Then they beam at you with them eyes!

And that's not to even *mention* what comes out of their mouths! Each bloomin' one of them is a new compendium of word hoards. And *then* they tell *stories.* "How did she come up with that?"[2]

So for you, in your new writing group, or class, or clan, or cabal—the main thing you want is the absence of contraction and the maximum of generosity. And that's the main gift you want to give to others: expansion and openness. It's that openness that gives people the ability to come up with the right word, the word "haranguing" or "bozo" or "rutabaga." It gives people the perceptual capacity to come up with the brilliant plot twist in which their piteously stuck main character inexplicably makes just the right choice at just the right moment, leaving the homeless shelter with the millionaire crack heiress in the paisley convertible. Being open to the subconscious can do all that, and you want your writing group to help make that happen.

So here are some excellent principles for how to work together with other people so that all kinds of paisley goes off in everybody's mind.

---

[2] This book, by the way, is crowded with other people. Their wise and funny words and ideas are infiltrated throughout.

PARAMETER-KIND-OF-THING WHICH ISN'T
EXACTLY A SPECIFIC TECHNIQUE NUMBER
THIRTY-SEVEN

Gentle and Generous Principles of Working with Other People (or, how to deal with the other rutabagas)

So there's the thing called a writing group. We can agree it exists? You can do it in a church basement, you can meet in a cafe, an open living room. Maybe you've got the bravura to teach your own writing class. People working together, doing freewrites together, handing out drafts to bring home and mark, reading pieces out loud. Here are some big important principles to prevent owies and channel up the subconscious:

BE GENEROUS. Generosity has many good effects. When listening, remember yourself—and be forthgoing to remind others—that this is about gift giving. Amazing how easy it is to forget that someone has reached into some interior space, expending effort on the emotional, psychic, and sometimes even spiritual plane, to bring forth and read to you some act of the creative and expressive self. Remember the generosity, and be generous in return. Acknowledge the gift of their risking their interior amoeba in the tempestuous waters and general fracas of the World. Say "Thank you!" Say it a lot.

BE GENEROUS TO YERSELF, TOO. Before you read your piece to the group, none of this, "Well, it's not very good," or "It's not as good as that last one," or "It's disorganized," or "The only reason it's like this is because *blah blah blah* . . ." Not only is this not interesting, and uncomfortable for others to listen to, it robs you of the width of feedback you *could* get by framing the piece for other people. They will then listen to your piece against the question: "Well, is it *really* blah blah blah?" They will be constructing reasons to prove to you that it *isn't* disorganized, or that it *is* as good as the last one, etc. This means that they aren't fully listening to it. You have corralled off their possible responses (which are almost infinite) to "agree-disagree" or "prove-disprove." This not only robs them of possible ways to experience your piece, but it also robs you of a more open-ended kind of feedback.

always take care of yourself

DO NOT INTERPRET OR PSYCHOANALYZE. This is not a joke. One night, years back, I had a class, and a man said (and this was the first night of our group) after a woman had read her work, "You're really on a control trip, aren't you?"

OK, that's an obvious one, and so baldly lacking in kindness. But actually, most analyzing of a piece *reduces* it. The piece is full of possibilities: delicious lies that might be true, points of contact between the ecosystem and the heart-break, descriptions of how dread feels from the inside while Ruth is looking at the gym floor in seventh grade. And if someone in your group says "Oh, I know how *you* felt; I was insecure too," there's just a huge minusing that's happening to the piece.

First: Ruth ain't necessarily the same person as the "you" author person who wrote that scene. Second: It might not even be *about* insecurity. And even if it *is* about insecurity, it surely isn't *only* about insecurity. When someone reduces it by interpreting it, a theme or idea takes over ("insecurity") and diminishes the way the golden boards of the basketball court feel buttery and also subaqueous as Ruth looks down into them.

Don't even interpret in a praisy way, "Oh, I loved how you evoked the pathos of the narrator." It's another diminishment. Especially don't psychoanalyze. No one signed up for that. And even if you *are* a therapist by profession (in which case you probably already know this), people haven't come to a writing group to let someone have a crack at teasing apart their psyches in front of everyone.

Well then, you might say, What way *do* you give feedback? Well, there's *lots* of good ways, and I delightedly talk about that below, in Readback-Feedback and in Impressionisms, but we're trying to stay organized here (even me!), staying with the Principles.

DON'T TELL OTHER PEOPLE HOW TO FIX THEIR PIECE.

"Raise the emotional stakes," said one online writing teacher about one of my students' pieces of fiction. He came to me asking whether he had "raised the emotional stakes." Another student had been told by a Poetry Professor that she must speed up the pace. It's like professional parenting gurus. My mother told me that her mother only fed her every four hours when she was an infant, because Gran had read in a book that that's the way to feed a baby properly. It was the new Scientific Method of 1929 and she followed it, even though it broke her heart to hear the baby scream. One book on How to Write says to include colors and the time of day in your piece, another says to use short sentences, another says to use long sentences. Another says to write only from the meditative place of mind. Are we inscribing this in the big leather-bound book of Great Big Writing Truths or something? Are we making writing the way Henry Ford makes cars on the assembly line? "Raise the emotional stakes, slow down, speed up, lie down, roll over, shake!" Gag me with a dog biscuit.

Sure, you can *try* all kinds of Ways to Write, and you should. There are lots of cool techniques and tricks. But writing shouldn't be theory-driven. To write better, what you need to do is to write more like you.

DON'T MAKE IT ABOUT COMPETITION AND WHO IS "A WRITER." A writing group that supports the subconscious is not another forum for survival of the fittest. See, we've got a problem in our culture that comes out of a linguistic confusion. Because there are two meanings, really different meanings, trying to cram themselves into one word. The word is "writer." One meaning is "Important professional person who is officially Creative and is paid *money* to put words on paper." They have been Published. They are a rock star. They are better than you. They are an archetype! If they are men, all women smile at them. If they are women, everyone thinks their hair looks *great!* They can say, "I am a writer," at cocktail parties. (Does anyone even *go* to cocktail parties anymore?) They have an editor and an agent. ("My agent said . . .")

The other meaning of "writer," the meaning of "writer" in this book, is someone who writes. Do you write? You are a writer. Let's get over it. We can just define those people who make their living at writing as "people who make their living at writing."[3]

But the thing that causes suffering and pain (which is what I'm concerned with here) in the attempt to evaluate "Who is a real Writer" is the *comparing*. Trying to outdo each other pours Miracle Grow on the insecurity, and, as I do keep saying, these experiments, these Gateways to the Subconscious work when you remain open, and watching, and delighted. And that isn't about contraction.

What you want to do is *enjoy* writing. Even if you *are* trying to get famous, or write about an important subject,

[3] In case you are tempted to glamorize that life, being a paid writer is a lot of stress. One person I know writes corporate reports for a living. Another person I know writes travel books for a living. A third writes magazine articles for a living. Most of them talk about never being able to come up for air: they have a deadline. They have to hustle new work. They have to sacrifice their principles. "I'm sorry, too busy to hang out with you. I've gotta get this piece in . . ."

like Race and Class Politics in Silicon Valley, the writing will be better if you learn to enjoy writing. And that happens best if you are not trying to compete.[4]

WRITE ABOUT *ANYTHING* **YOU WANT.** Which also means, **YOU NEVER HAVE TO READ YOUR PIECE OUT LOUD IF YOU DON'T WANT TO.** It's important to write about what you want to write about. What if you want to write about menstruation and everybody else in the room is a guy? What if you are absolutely sick of your elderly parent's Alzheimer's ravings and insults but (you are thinking as you write), who can criticize a helpless and sick person like that? What if one person in your group is really uptight about masturbation, and you want to write about how good it feels? What if you've been weeping about your friend's desertion and you want to write about it, but you're just not up for more weeping right now, which might happen if you read it?

Just tell yourself, "I can write about anything, and I when it comes to my turn to read, I can just say 'I pass.'" You may change your mind when it comes around to your turn to read, but while you're writing it, just keep that option open. If you feel like there is social pressure to read, then there will be a lot of stuff you won't allow out of your pen, and that's the exact opposite of what you want to do.

TAKE YOUR TIME. Your writing group is your time. An unhurried time. You've made a space in your crash-and-burn life for a writing group and the last thing you want to do is to turn it into another rigidly-curtailed, agenda-driven paragon of efficiency. Slow down. If it takes someone a long time to read his piece, that's *good*. Sink into it. It's good for your health to gaze into space.

---

[4] OK, yes, if you crush the other people in your group and you let them know that in fact you are the meanest dog in town, there is that "thrill of victory" thing, and maybe you can enjoy that. *But in your writing group?*

It's also good for you to read your own piece slowly. I know, I know, "It's really not that good, so if I just speed up and rush through it maybe they won't notice how awful it is, and it's actually considerate of me to speed up so I don't take up their time with me and seem arrogant and selfish to boot."

But can't you see how *wrong* that is? *You* may be familiar with the piece, having written it, but *they've* never heard it before. It takes time for them to not only decode it and relate it to what you read a second ago, but also (important!) they need the space for *them* to live in it themselves. Hurrying isn't being considerate; it's the opposite. Try listening to someone else's piece all rushed up and you'll see what I mean.

And you don't have to read your piece in some unnatural way, all slo-o-owed down like a 45 record played at 33 and 1/3. Just pause between phrases. Pause longer than that. Longer than you would. Everyone else could use time to breathe, too. You are helping them to slow down, which, as you know, they need to do.

IF YOU DON'T WANT TO DO THE SAME EXERCISE AS EVERYBODY ELSE, DON'T. So you've gotten together to do writing. Someone has thought up a topic. "Let's write about bread!" Sounds good. And you start. Then you remember something. It doesn't have to do with bread. A memory has come up from a dream and you don't want to lose it. Or on your way over tonight you saw your old lover on the sidewalk and she crossed the street to avoid you. You know you need write about this now. So write about it. And since everybody else in your group has read the same principles and agreed upon them in a groovy consensus fashion, you don't need to apologize, "Well, it's not really about bread . . . but . . . sorry," burying your face in your hands with shame . . . Forget it! Write what you want.

Or what if somebody suggests that everyone does technique number ten (Counting Splice!) and says, "Let's shatter everything!" And you're like "Wait . . . wait . . . but!" Because you want to be in the redwoods of your mind. The time in the morning just after dawn when the sunlight was slanting through the huge trees, steaming the rainwater off the electric-green moss. You do not want to shatter and scramble it. So don't. Do something else. Follow your pleasure.

Writing is better when you seek your own pleasure and enjoyment.

Do everything you want and nothing you don't.

ACTUAL FUN THING TO DO WITH OTHER PEOPLE NUMBER THIRTY-EIGHT

Word Kleptocracy[5]

Hey, Mr. A, how about an actual exercise to do with each other?[6]

OK! This one's a big, deep confounding of one of our most sacred truths about writing. You know: "This has to make sense." It also monkey-wrenches another unquestioned assumption in writing, which is "It's mine." Word Kleptocracy is a randomizer. And it connects you to each other. How full! And it's a legitimizing of larceny. That's right, this book gives you permission.

TRY IT!

Someone suggests a topic for the group. (I know, *Writing Open the Mind* does not ask people to write on a specific topic. But even *Writing Open the Mind* has to break its own rules.) People throw out ideas: Let's all write about the inner critic! Or closets! Or dirty sex! Or the sacred!

Whatever it is, experiment with saying "Yes." Yes makes things simpler in this life. Saying "No" is blocking. Try Yes. In

---

[5] Thanks to Keith Hennessy for the clue for this one!

[6] A lot of the experiments so far can be done with others, and some of them can be combobulated differently with groups.

improv theater, this is called the "Yes, let's!" principle. *Or*, if you just don't want to, everyone can write on different topics. Kleptocracy still works. This is not a political summit meeting on limiting intercontinental ballistic missiles. Do what you want to.

But you do decide to do a fast freewrite, seven minutes, nonstop. And—here's the fun part—you are going to steal. You sit next to each other, really close in a circle, maybe even on the floor. Close enough so that you can see the paper of the person to your right and the person to your left without having to move. If your handwriting is messy (my handwriting is messy), print in big block letters or something. You've got to be readable.

So . . . Start writing! Then, whenever you feel like it (but often), look to your left, or right, and *steal their words*. That's right. Intellectual property is *so* flushed down the toilet. It's as if it didn't even exist. This is good. You look at that person's page, catch a phrase, and *copy it down on your page right next to whatever your last word was*. Like it was part of the same sentence. In fact, it *is* part of the same sentence. Then keep writing your own words. Keep writing. Now, twelve seconds later (or whenever—but really really often) look right. Or left. And steal some more. You can't make out the word exactly? *It doesn't matter!* Make up the word you *think* it is. Don't interrupt with speaking. Let the transpersonhood unfold. Write as fast (legibly now!) as you can. Keep going. Steal right and left at unpredictable intervals. Do it a lot, say 60 percent of the words on your page are not yours. Don't try to make it fit grammatically. Forget about sense.

Yes, you will get scrambled. That's part of the point. It will go in a different direction than you planned. Another part of the point. Other people are a wonderful source of the unpredictable. You don't like that word he just used? Oh well. Write it down. Let it affect you, and plow right on ahead. You might start laughing. Laughing is good, but keep right on writing. Let the words go around. And around.

Finish! Ring the bell.

Now everyone read! And watch what has happened.

Hey, These **QUESTIONS FOR THE CURIOUS,**—We Could Talk about Them Together![7]

Did you see words go around? Migrating, interpenetrating? Trendy lit-crit types call this being "interwritten by texts." How cool. How good. Did your grand plans for direction get hopelessly stymied? A scramble a day keeps the critic at bay.

THE MIND OF IT:

You can remember that this is a great way to find a place inside you that does not heed the calls to order. If you discover the disorder of this funhouse mirror, you can slip it in your hip pocket and take it with you everywhere. Start changing direction without a visible sense of purpose at any old time. It's a *very* nifty device.

CONJURING THE SUBCONSCIOUS IN OTHERS WITHOUT EVEN TRYING NUMBER THIRTY-NINE

Readback-Feedback: Fertilizing Others' Writing without Hijacking Their Work

So Peppermint Patty, Yosemite Sam, Barney Rubble, Foghorn Leghorn, Betty, Veronica, Jughead, and a couple of Power Rangers are in the rec-room in the basement. They've finished a freewrite and they've just read the Gentle and Generous Principles and think that they are great. Now they're ready to "fertilize others' writing without hijacking their work," whatever that is. Someone said something about "Readback-Feedback," but didn't tell them what it was.

[7] You can talk about lots of the questions in this book together, go back and try them out. What do the other critters say?

Foghorn reads his piece, and while he reads, everyone else copies down some of his words—ones they responded to—as is. Peppermint Patty chose those particular words and phrases because . . . well, she doesn't know exactly, but she responded to them. That's good. Maybe she liked them, or maybe the sounds of the words gave her the creeps. She wrote those words down. The idea scratched some itch. She wrote the words down. The end of one phrase and the beginning of the next made her imagination kink. She wrote that down.

When you write down people's words, yours is not to wonder why. If it evokes a response, you write it down. You don't change the order, or try to make it tricky, or do some sort of end-run interpretation of the piece. You just respond and write down. You are not, however, a stenographer: write down five or twelve phrases, here and there, as you listen. The gaps between will be the words you didn't write down.

And don't interrupt Foghorn as he reads his piece (except to ask him to *please slow down*. Remind him that you are not a stenographer.)

When Foghorn is finished, Veronica and the Power Rangers and Peppermint Patty, everyone, one by one, reads back to Foghorn whatever they wrote down, and nothing else. No reasons why they chose that word or this. No, "Wow, you're such a great writer." They start as soon as Foghorn is finished reading, (no pause to clap or query) one by one, and Foghorn just listens. People do not say, "This was nicer than that." Not "I didn't like the part about the fried chicken." Not "That was really avant garde." Just read his words back, and nothing else.[8]

And if, this time, it's your turn to have your words read back to you, you just listen: let them wash over the consciousness, listening for gaps, connections, and pictures floating to mind. See what it's like, especially the differences from one person to the next. Don't be all nervous, or try to figure out which parts were

---

[8] There's a reason for this, but instead of bogging you down with Ideas, let's just see how it feels when it happens to you.

good, or analyze why Peppermint Patty chose that phrase. Let it all go. Don't freak out about how terrible it was, or how you wish you hadn't read that part. Try to really hear. Don't miss out on what's happening in their choosings and gaps. See how closely you can perceive. This is another and entirely different experience of the subconscious. Feel what it feels like.

So, after everybody has read back Foghorn's words, it's his chance to talk about what happened, again without other people barging in and telling him what his piece was or wasn't. They're too interested anyway to find out what he discovered. What *was* it like? He gives his report from the inside: the pilgrimage from writing the freewrite, to reading it out loud, to getting the Readback-Feedback. The people in the group heard only the results of the journey—that is, the words that came out—but Foghorn felt the journey itself. The words were the *accessories* to the crime—the crime itself was deep inside his cartoony brain. What were the thoughts and emotions that flitted through the mind? Little voices saying this or that? Imaginations of something completely else?

**Noticing is good.
Tell us what you noticed.**

Did the words seem to shift in their feeling tones and meanings in the three cycles—writing it, reading it, and hearing it back? The words were the same, but the experience was different. When certain words are haiku'd out, new linkages happen. Was there anything interesting in the particular gaps? Or in the differences between each person's reading back to you?

While you speak, everyone else just listens, hears what happened to you along the way. Then, when the first reader has finished talking of his experience, the next one reads her freewrite, and she gets to bathe in this generous bouillabaisse of appreciation too. You find the path through the forest of your own work through the minds of your friends.

The more times you do this the deeper it works.

THE MIND OF IT (OR, BUT WHAT ABOUT ALL THAT LITERARY STUFF?):

I know you could talk about the style and pace and theme and plot. Those things "exist" and you've got your ideas about how they relate to Foghorn's piece. You want to *help* him. You've got *ideas* to transmit.

That's cool and all—and you could even try that some other time—but first see what happens to Foghorn's view of his own piece as it gets transmitted back in gists. A lot more information is communicated than you'd probably think.

AMAZING INTERACTIVE FREEWRITEY THING TO DO WITH OTHER PEOPLE NUMBER FORTY

Gift Economy: Re-sequencing Via the Kaleidoscope Sunglasses of Others

When you listen to another person's work, you are like a Polynesian mariner, finding yourself on an unknown shore. This person's interior is as wild as the island of Borneo, and as basically unknown. It's a land exotic with plumed tapirs, aqueous leopards, and airborne snakes. You cannot go farther in than the shoreline. At the wide estuary where you have stationed your beechbark canoe, a river of language pours out from a Far Back that you cannot know. In Readback-Feedback, you collected driftwood and hubcaps and a broken piece of painted oar passing you by. You gathered a starfish, a roof tile, a mask. Up the river are the twisted mangrove swamps and the high, jungly mountains rolling back into the unseen.

The land is The Other, your friend, that critter there on the sofa all innocent-looking with her pen. You meet her on the shore. She is delighted and amazed at the pieces of the interior you plucked from the flow. Each of your collected artifacts that washed down the river hints at the complex civilization thriving in the highland valleys and the windswept ridges.

In Gift Economy, you are sitting on the beach, poking with your finger at the driftwood and conch shells, the words you collected, and you think, "I wonder what they would look like if I put them together this way? Or this?" You become lost in a reverie, putting the painted oar in the middle of a circle of chipped clay figurines facing outwards. (You are not bringing the pink paper Mai Tai umbrellas from your world here: just messing around rearranging what is already here.) Now you hang the hubcaps from the bamboo sticks—just so—and they reflect the purple rays of the tropical sun.

What is your gift here? The gift is the gift of re-patterning, hallowed be its name. You put these language artifacts together in a new place or way and you give your friend a gift that she cannot give herself. She then goes back into the interior, bringing seven long blue feathers and a handful of brown and white beads. She posts them around and between the starfish and the mask, like sentries in repose.

TRY IT! (OR ROBERT'S RULES OF DISORDER)

In listening to each person's work in Readback-Feedback (the previous mongoose), you crossed the ocean between the two of you and collected the artifacts at the mouth of their river, and now they're living there on the pages in front of you. We'll be using those fragments you've collected here in Gift Economy. You have the opportunity to bestow the immaterial (but potent) boon of re-sequencing on the person of your friend to the right by repatterning those nuggets of phrases and thought. On your left, the unknowable field of turbulence that goes by the name "guy in your writing group" will be doing this for you. For the Borneo of you.

So, for this one you will need to have already done Readback-Feedback, and you'll also need some of those moveable agents of disorder-reorder, those redoubtable shamans, the index cards. What you'll do is use those previous nuggets of phrases from Readback-Feedback and you choose seven of the phrases (short ones) from the person on your right, then copy them down on seven cards, one nugget per card, just as they were.

Now here's the gift: move them around in the river of time, which is to say, put them in a new order. Avoid trying to be "tricky" and avoid going for "flow." You are showing something new to the mind of your friend. You don't explain; you just re-sequence the cards, and hand the cards back to the critter who wrote them. The person on your left hands yours to you.

Without further ado, you all lay your cards out in front of you, some instigator rings the bell, and you begin now to write. Twenty minutes is good. You want the new order to move you, so don't be pre-conceived. Let intuition—and the new story that suggests itself—fill in the blanks. You write in between the lines. You see what occurs.

QUESTIONS FOR THE CURIOUS (QUESTIONY-QS):

Did you see a different story in the new sequence? Could you sense some not-quite-explicable intention in the sequence you received? I think of the re-sequencing as a kind of a gift because your partner has shown you new things in the links between cards. It's incredible how little it takes. Where does the intention of the gift-giving live? In the blanks between cards?

THE MIND OF IT:

In Readback-Feedback, the pieces you collected and gave back came in a sequential fall of dominoes, one after the other. And, even with their gaps, their linkings maintained the original chain of thought that led the writer, again and again, to her inevitable conclusions. To her, it seemed seamless. But you knew that it wasn't. You weren't invested in the picture sequence that the words came from. Those words were comfy in their persuasive little home, just the way they were. But you—the foreign mariner—weren't invested in the pitter-patter that links first to the next.

Of course she could have re-sequenced the phrases for herself. But that wouldn't be the same. Here we have a different way to see provided by another intelligence (you), whose life has intersected with hers for reasons impossible to know. Each person you meet can be the harbinger of the unanticipated, the person to make Known things into New.

Mike Pelton, a carpenter, said once, "I never realized books were like houses, that you could take a wall out here and put a sliding glass door in there, a staircase in the middle. I thought books were permanent things, just like they are when you buy them." Your friend resequencing your phrases opened a window in the middle of a wall. You saw only plastered-over sheetrock, a blank face of inevitability. She, however, hooked her fingers under the sash (there's a sash there?!), threw open the blinds, and let in the air.

Does the journey end here? Why should it? The piece of writing in your hand is forever renewable, forever alive. It can be re-sequenced again and again. Should writing have an end? Ari Gold, a seventh-grade English teacher, tells his students that there's a poet who revised a poem nine hundred times. Perhaps for Ari this is to show the tykers that revision is a thing that normal people do. For me, it howls with the great and wild truth that a work can be—if we are really, really open—never totally Done.

REVISIONISTIC-MYSTICAL EXCHANGE
BETWEEN PEOPLE NUMBER FORTY-ONE

Object Transmutation

We change writing. We revise writing, we fix writing, we edit writing, re-sequence writing, give it a different slant or stance. A piece grows bigger and smaller. We change our mind and put it back the way it was. All of this stuff that we do to a piece of writing can be put under a macro-mega header called "transformation." Mostly our own writing gets transformed by ourselves: scratch out this word and put in another. Try a different beginning. Move stuff around. But then, there are those times when the transformation happens with other folkses. If someone is an editor of your work, and they've got the upper hand of power, it might be shaped according to their goals and tastes. Your piece is under the scalpel of their whims and predilections. But that's when there's a power imbalance. What about collaborative writing? Comrade A: "Hmm, what if we put in Natasha's name here, instead of 'she'"? Comrade B: "Yeah, that's good! But let's call her Sasha." Comrade A: "Yeah."

The thing about all of these transformations is that they come from the front of the brain. In transforming from the subconscious, you are stretching, sideways, toward some other else. Usually you do this subconscious subduction in your own private solar system. This time you will be aided and abetted by the critters by your side.

Remember the incense whiffs, aroma shiftings, and dilations by sound in Sway? This is like Sway, but with the fourth dimension added in. Other people are your fourth dimension. In Object Transmutation, you offer the other people in your group a new whiff of their piece, a whiff of your Okefenokee tidewaters for their wind-swept plains.

TRY IT!

We're gonna use stuff, physical objects for this. Quite a number of them. Whose house are you at? Will she let you raid her kitchen drawers and cabinets for utensils, let you paw through her curiosity cabinet for little clay statuettes? Or perhaps you decide ahead of time that you'll will bring things over from your houses, or pinecones and orange blossoms from your yards. You could even add a secretive element: bring these things over in a brown paper bag and don't show others what you brought.

What kinds of things could you bring? Anything. Objects: lipstick, a wrench, a doll, jumper cables. A can of baked beans. Don't show them! Keep your beans close to your chest.

You start after you've all read aloud a freewrite or a piece you've brought in, and everybody is open to trying a transformation. You've all signed the liability waiver and are ready to let go and release your exclusive ownership of what the piece will turn into being. Check and agree.

So this is what you will do. You heard Bob's freewrite, and he's sitting there on your right. You have your bag of Symbolic Items. Thinking sweetly and/or mischievously, you select five objects in advance for Bob that in some way may give him a clue or twinge about a transformation he could do to his piece. Felipe, on your left, has heard your piece. He's ready with his five, coming at you. Someone's got a timer set for four minutes and will set it to "ding."

You're gonna re-inhabit the topic of the piece you just read aloud and transform it into something new through this object transmutation. When the bell rings, Felipe will hand you an object, and you hand one to Bob. You hold it in one hand, write with the other. Your pen is moving and you're holding . . . a Smurf! Let the Smurf drench your art (which is to say mind) until the timer says "ding."

So, from Felipe, after the Smurf, (set the timer each round), you get a bottle of men's cologne, then a power drill, then a Cuban cigar, and . . . a barbecue fork. You didn't expect *that*. (Thank you, other critters, for fritzing my brain!) You smile to yourself, imagining Bob's delight at being handed the pacifier, the toy soldier, the shovel, the fireplace poker, and the photo of Sue.

Again, might I say, as in Sway, you aren't writing *about* the Smurf, but letting something connected to the Smurf, or the aura surrounding the Smurf, or the feeling and memory spurred on by the Being of the Smurf, have hintings and hueings on the way the words emerge from the pen.

Everybody ready? Pens held aloft? Write for four minutes, until that timer goes ding. Then you get another Thing, and the timer starts again. Five objects, five views, four minutes each.

QUESTIONS FOR THE CURIOUS:

Did you get some object, perhaps, that you didn't "like"? That you didn't know what to do with? What did you do with it? Maybe you were forced to extemporize, make some quack you had no intention of making? When the improviser's mind is ready to say "Yes," the herky-jerky of non-conceptual sideways connection aligns with the whosits-whatzits of the whole wide world. It does. Now.

THE MIND OF IT:

Congratulations, you are a vector in the grand dance of the unforeseen. You are spiking the punch of someone else's prom. You are giving them an Ultraman when before they only had Speed Racer and Underdog. The puzzle piece you give them puzzles their piece. *That* they had not thought to do. Please be the spanner in their works. They will thank you for your gifts.

GENIE NUMBER FORTY-TWO

Impressionisms: Giving Feedback from the Interior, Guess-Making Mind

What's the big difference between, "There's a lot of passive voice in this middle section here. You should change it to active," and "When I read 'lounging half-animal,' I thought about my brother and how he would wheeze into his beer"? One is an urban traffic-flow control system designed by well-meaning bureaucrats. And the other is a movie of the mind.

When you read or listen to someone else's piece, you imagine. The words run amok in your mind. You make new things with someone else's words, and throw in your own wheezing beer brother, Polynesian mariner, Etruscan urn, annoyance at mixed metaphors . . . and push "play."

On the other side of the equation, when *you've* written some words and let them off the page, and out of your mouth, and into someone else's berserk machine, there's no *telling* what they'll do with them. They're your words and now the foreigners have got hold of them. What barbarian practices are they doing with them in that far away place, in that Paris of their minds? Do they roll the dice and play Parcheesi with them? Do they put them on like a mask and dance in front of a fire? Do they float lazily down the river on the raft of them? Do they hang them in their Left Bank confrontational art gallery and talk about the inexplicable soul of the Primitive who made them?

Readback-Feedback gave you a bunch of hints about what happened back in the catacombs of your listeners when you read them your piece. But perhaps you have a sense that there's more to discover about what happened inside them? Could people possibly respond to each other's pieces from the same place of mystical association that they write from, from the Subconscious Itself?

TRY IT!

Giving Impressionistic feedback means that you give another person a movie of your internal subjective experience of reading or listening to their work. Simple is good. Generosity is the touchstone. No need (and no good) to say what the piece "is." Please avoid any "You are this," or "You are that." You listen to your friend's piece, and your subliminal self issues reports of what happened inside you. It's not about him. What did *you* experience? Be idiosyncratic. Where did your memory go? What did you see?

Impressionistic feedback says, "When I heard this specific part, I felt *this*. I imagined *this*. I remembered *this*." Here's what it's like: "When I heard the part about 'We're like little children, writing our names with sparklers at night . . . but seconds later they're gone,'[9] I felt a wave of loneliness and at the same time a sense of magic, but a magic that is available to other people, not to me." That is to say, impressionistic feedback is a precisely-noticed set of impressions of what happened in your mind.

The writing made an impression, and you share that impression.

You can report from your wanting: "I wanted to know more about the silences inherited by your grandmother." You can report from your emotional world: "I wanted to cry." You can speak from an inexplicable place: "I wanted to erect an obelisk in a wide grassy field." And you tell exactly *when* you wanted it. "When I heard the part about the 'Cyclops of intention,' I wanted to erect an obelisk in a wide grassy field."

You don't have to explain *why* you want to erect the obelisk. You do not have to evaluate, analyze, cite facts, studies, authorities. Do not say to the reader that Faulkner *and* the Dalai Lama

[9] Adam Kinsey

both agree with her and her Main Point. Of course do not judge. Do not say, "I thought the part about the Cyclops was weird." Do not say, "Was that Cyclops a metaphor for your mental illness?" Do not even say "Was that Cyclops a metaphor for the criminal justice system in this country?" (Just because someone's read you their piece, it doesn't mean they wanna chat about the content.) And *definitely* avoid like the plague, "When you expressed your attraction to the Cyclops, I really understood where you were coming from." (The "I" in the piece is always "the narrator," not "you.") Instead, give back generously to the people who were kind enough to read you their work, to give you a little window into the inside of their self.

> "It made me think of my Pa."

So whadda we do again?

• Notice your desires for the piece, but don't give instructions.

• Give the movie of your mind, not pronouncements on what the piece "is." What did it do to the inside of you?

• Appreciate. Specifically. Go as micro (in your interior experience) as you possibly can.

• Allow the writer to get dangerous: don't pin down an "I." (Allow the "Who is the 'You?'" to not have an answer.)

If you are the writer getting feedback, you can choose some of these questions to have asked of your piece:

• How did you feel when reading this paragraph/page?

• Which parts did you remember?

• What did the ending do to you?

• Were there parts that surprised you?

• When I read _____ , I thought/remembered/felt _____ .

• What do you sense is the source of energy/center of gravity here?

• Describe the texture(s) you feel in the piece.

Or you may just want people to tell you where they responded to it, and that's all. There's a time in the process for that: don't underestimate it. And think how much more free the other writers in your group will feel after you unabashedly say, "Just tell me where you like it."

THE MIND OF IT:

Why so careful?

We do this so carefully because mysterious happenings don't like bright lights being shone on them, or scalpels, or blueprints, and because in freewriting we want to encourage the *writer* to be free. Your primary goal is to help the writer keep writing. That will help her more than any fixing of this specific piece.

And OK, yes, as the writer you *can* ask other people to tell you what to do, or to give you their judgements: "This part doesn't work for me," etc. But be sure that's what you want, and that you are at the right stage of the process to get that kind of feedback. And if you haven't yet experienced Only Impressionism, just try it first and see how it feels.

Does this kind of feedback really work?

So you might say, "But I can *see* that this transition here is incoherent and disjointed, and you are telling me that I'm not supposed to help the person?"

Well, for one thing, maybe the writer is going for a disjointed feeling, and you don't know that. Secondly, maybe you can't immediately see the coherence, but you might later see it when you've read the piece twice, or are in a more subtle mood. Or maybe it "is" disjointed, but fixing it for someone, especially if that's not what they wanted, can spook the thread of their writing trance, and it might not be what they need.

The most important thing, the most soulful thing about this kind of feedback, however, is that when you trust another person, the writer you are giving your response to, there's room in her to connect to a little locusty part in herself, all silver-green wings and night rattle. When you let her into your own colonnade of associations and memories, then she gets more of how to do that with herself. She connects with the parts of her writing that for unknown reasons rocked your soul in the bosom of Abraham, and that allows her to connect with the quadrant of herself that wrote it. That sector, the one that hates searchlights and sirens and rulers, is magical, wise, and inexplicable. Your feedback helps her conscious, Right Now mind (the one that's listening to you) connect to the skittery locust mind, so that she can do it again next time, easier and easier, more and more and more.

Take the long view, and the writing grows more. Because it grows from inside.

Inventing Your Own Experiments: Some Theory for This Practice

Well . . . cool. Games, Theories, Maelstroms, Provisos, Party Hats, Seaweed, Balloon Guys twisting out balloon dachshunds, and Moving Like a Villain. Who knew this was all in writing? But we did know it was in consciousness. And if something exists in consciousness, it can exist there with writing.

There are lots of different soil nutrients that went into developing this kind of work for me, perhaps starting from my first remembering of dreams, or from meeting Carm, the appliance repair guy who came by our suburban house in Illinois when I was eleven and started telling me about hypnosis and took me to a hypnosis symposium. And ever since then, through improv theater play, meditation, living deep in nature, and goofing around with language, this has all come together. This kind of work has taken form in the very way I hyperventilatingly advocate throughout this book: Follow your own interests and curiosities; experiment with ideas instead of trying to force them into some pre-conceived mold; be open to possibilities and surprises coming out of nowhere; freewrite and try to see how free that could be; and be open to the "where did *that* come from" place, wherever that is. (And I still do not know.)

And I'll say too that I'm grateful to have been able to learn myself how to write from the subconscious. It's opened up my way of being in the world. I keep discovering that Buddhist truth about the lack of solidity in the world, but in a circus kind of way, even though it seems to be the tendency of my body, or the influence of society, or both, to get myself all boarded up again and again. But messing around with *this* stuff, every time I get a chance to freewrite, or to teach a class, I get to re-open myself, continually, to the possibility-drenched universe. So I know that it's good. I give it to you.

This book, also, was written in the same way I trumpet in its pages: Messing around. Letting things converge and grow. Adding and subtracting. Lots of resequencing. Lots of letting ideas and hunches grow. Trying out different versions. And also from tuning into parts where the energy seemed to rise, to centers of gravity, and from letting go of the rest. Revisions and Re-Visions.

And also part of this stuff came from studying in a more formal way and thinking on top of the shoulders of people who came before. I went and got a master's degree in teaching writing, and though the goals of most English composition programs are quite different from mine, I owe the people who trained me in that world a great debt. I also owe a debt to the aesthetics of Japan, where I lived for many years. I spent a lot of time there looking at flower arrangements, known as *ikebana*, which is really a system of putting things together—in this case flowers—that allows the viewer to enter in. I thought, What would it be to write this way? Open-endedly? In a few more pages, I'll give you little sketch-drawings of some of the trains of thought that fertilized this work—ikebana, hermeneutics, affirmative inquiry, postmodernist thought—so that, if you want to, you can grow your own writing experiments from the same rich loam. If you are into thinky kinds of things, you can read those sketches, and then if you get a wild hair to do so, scour up more information from the multiplicitous world of facts and ideas.

But before those sketches, I'd like to just say that you can reach into your own hoard of knowledge and experience to make up your own experiments and games in writing and consciousness. The basic idea is that you can use so many things of this world to sway your mindstate, or to scramble your text, or to oscillate between or push against, or to provide you with allegory and imagery, or to translate through your body, or to give you word sounds, or to find inner and outer voices to add to your mix, or to help you re-see or revise. The world is full of many things. And so is your mind.

Here are some thoughts just to get you started. What if you went to the zoo with a pad of paper, started to imitate an animal with your physical body, and then wrote from that place? Or if you are a psychologist, instead of writing through genres, you could write through the lenses of the different diagnoses of the DSM IV. Or if it's chakras you know about, have them converse, or write in their voices. Or you could use the fact that there are so many different types of people in the world, and so many ways of classifying those types. Write through the viewpoints of the different astrological signs (Chinese or Western). I don't know a lot about them, but maybe you do, and thus that gateway can be yours. Jungian personality types, the nine Enneagram types, the different constitutional characteristics of people in Ayurvedic or homeopathic medicine, or the seven habits of highly successful climbers. You can write from inside the fortress of any of them, then move outside and look in. Juxtapose one against another and see how they collide. Bring your own knowledge to this. If it happens in your brain or your body, or the natural world, you can let it affect your writing.

Maybe you do Jungian sand tray therapy for a living. Maybe you study death and dying and give people guidance on grieving. Maybe you lead racial justice and reconciliation trainings and use those tools and techniques. Maybe you do sound healing. Bring it all to this work.

And, Yes, you can write *about* all those things, but you can also try writing about all the phenomena of this world and your life *through the lenses* of each of these viewpoints on reality, these places of mind that sound healing or jazz dance or zoo animals bring out in you. Each way of using the mind is different, and I've given you just a few tastes. Please grow your own, and experiment.

An example might be this: You're a neurologist and you have your techie gadget machines that allow you to activate different sectors of the brain, your brain, through electrode stimulation on different parts of the forehead. I don't know. You're the neurologist. Write about raising your daughter, or your trip to the Congo, or your photography artwork, through Alpha and Delta states that you induce with your machine: each of these Peepholes into the mystery of existence is distinct and has its own system of knowing the world, its own way of constellating the contents of consciousness, and thus each can sway the place that you write from. Inexhaustible and new.

I'll give you my own constellations here, below, and you can read them if you are curious, or you can jump right in and start cobbling your own. Please enjoy this world, and spread your excitement to others.

Asking Questions of the Good: Appreciative Inquiry

Appreciation makes you feel good. Appreciation helps the writer write well. There's a simplicity in this.

Specific appreciation shows a writer which parts of her piece of writing gave juice to the reader. It has the ability to cue the place in the subconscious mind of the writer that produced the resonant piece of writing, and by activating this area of the brain, make it stronger.

Appreciation is simple.

So what is the psychology of affirmation? I have only begun to explore its implications. My own impetus for writing and thinking about it comes from my experience of seeing criticism shut many writers up. I have always thought tearing into people about their writing was wrong, and I ranted against it, so it delighted me to find that out there in the business and nonprofit world, people were cooking with the same spices. In the rarified air of "organizational development," here were these other moles trying to bring more humanity to humans, and they called it Appreciative Inquiry. They were saying, "Don't look for problems, ask questions of the good." And intuitively, it makes sense.

But, you may say (and I may say) "Is it enough?" Well, it's true that asking other people if they thought this passage "worked" in your piece can sometimes be the most useful thing. Thinking out what you are trying to do in a piece is sometimes helpful, and you can ask "Did you feel invited into the piece?" (which could be answered with a yes or a no) or "Did it change moods suddenly?" And if they say, "Yeah, it did," then you have one piece of data. (Remember, maybe you wanted it to change moods suddenly.) You can ask about how a particular use of chronology worked out, or about the amount of characterization detail. But we have to protect our psyches from the cultural mania for criticism and make a fiery protest against attack-dog writing feedback. The buckshot method of "Just tell me what's wrong" is not the only route to grow in your writing. The interaction between two people around a piece of writing can be tremendously fertile; don't reduce it into an act of general unpleasantness for both.

What then is that alternative? David Cooperrider, the primary originator of Appreciative Inquiry, writes that it is less helpful to approach the world "as a problem to be solved":

> I am more effective, quite simply, as long as I can retain the spirit of inquiry of the everlasting beginner. The arduous task of intervention will give way to the speed of imagination and innovation; and instead of negation, criticism, and spiraling diagnosis, there will be discovery, dream, and design.

That's how they see it from the perspective of helping organizations grow and develop. How can you use it in your writing?

Asymmetry, Writing, and the Mind[1]

How does an artist or writer compose a work that is generous? How does a Japanese garden designer place a group of rocks together in a garden, and how do you put ideas and language next to each other on a page to invite a real participation? If you leave some of the connections unfinished, implied, you are, in one sense, giving a gift. When the composition is multifaceted, it offers a multitude of elements that combine in an abundance of ways.

A great teaching we can take from much East Asian art and poetry is that it does not force a particular interpretation, nor does it reveal all its secrets in a single viewing. The mind is refreshed and energized, and we feel invited inside.

In asymmetrical art or design, there is a differential of number or size or proportion. A lot of one thing, and a little of another. Elements clustered here, and not over there. Asymmetry is a counterpositioning of dissimilar—but not opposite—types. In asymmetrical design, the elements define a theatre, in the space of which an object or event of a different nature is intentionally placed. The tiniest thatched hut in the scope of vast forbidding mountains, the littlest smirk in the most serious of protests.

So, what is the connection between asymmetry and generosity? How does placing two dissimilar things against each other cause not only disjuncture but a feeling of space?

In *The Book of Tea*, a beautifully-written work published in 1906, painter, writer, and museum curator Okakura Kakuzo writes:

> The tea room is an 'Abode of the Unsymmetrical' inasmuch as it is consecrated to the worship of the Imperfect, purposely leaving something unfinished for the play of the imagination to complete.

[1] An earlier, longer version of this piece appeared in the magazine *Ikebana International*.

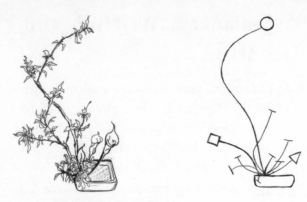

Asymmetry in Japanese flower arrangement.

Asymmetry in Japanese architecture.

In the tea room, in Chinese ink paintings, in the arrangement of rocks in a traditional Japanese garden, and in Japanese flower arrangement, asymmetry provokes the viewer's eyes to move about the piece. Thus asymmetrical design allows us to hint at something that is difficult to communicate in a straightforward manner, at an idea that can only be grasped from the side. Okakura Kakuzo again:

> In the tea room it is left for each guest in imagination to complete the total effect in relation to himself. The art of the extreme Orient has purposely avoided the symmetrical as expressing not only completion, but repetition. Uniformity of design was considered as fatal to the freshness of imagination.

When you write something, the sequence of sentences and paragraphs as they appear on the page reflects the movement of your thoughts. But it's more than reflection. Writing is creating, and words next to other words make fresh channels in the brain. And the fascinating thing is that this works backwards as well. You take different chunks of text, intentionally mix them, create new junctures, and new thinking appears. Or, if you juxtapose a narrative story with a dictionary definition, or sensory details with crisp dry assertions, or a proof with a rant, because these things feel "far" from each other, there is a sense of a gap. The mind begins to form guesses and suppositions. The synapses connect and energy is released.

Since each combination of these many dissimilar parts suggests its own meaning, its own interest and power, asymmetry in visual art or in writing encourages participation by the viewer or reader in the fertile process of creation. In this sense, writing asymmetrically is generous, because it gives the reader many different ways to understand, instead of insisting on one, one that is only our own. As Okakura Kakuzo writes,

> The dynamic nature of the Zen and Taoist philosophy laid more stress upon the process through which perfection was sought than upon perfection itself. True beauty could be discovered only by one who mentally completed the incomplete.

Clumping two things together that don't immediately make sense—it won't always "work." But asymmetry is about more than just the finished piece. Asymmetry is a process. It's a technique for thinking. It creates a new brain. Writing with generosity is letting go of a "one true meaning" that you must get across. You offer meaning in multiples, conjure new environments, and you let people go.

What Is Postmodernism, and Why Should I Care?

Well, it *is* part of the (semi-smug) hipness that postmodernist theory cloaks itself in to be complex and obscure and hard to "get." I've read tracts that claim that the whole *point* of postmodernist theory is that it is impossible to define. And here I am trying to define it. If you've ever tried to read it, you'll know that it comes with a lot of *baggage*. The writing about it is sometimes combative, and lots of people have their strong opinions about it. Or the sentences are so prickly and shape-shifting that nobody can figure out what those French theorists are saying. Or it just doesn't seem relevant.

Well, there are many little narratives inside me that agree with all that. And there's also another interior voice in here that says, Hey, this gaggle of ideas, "postmodernism," or "poststructuralism," can be liberating, could be healing, could make for fun writing games. And it has. Here is my idiosyncratic sketch-view of what it means, or what it could mean (sue me if I get it wrong):

The world is made up of a multiplicity of small stories, all coalescing, mixing, coming apart. You are a product of these stories. So is everyone else. A hundred thousand stories have come into you all your life: "One nation under God, indivisible," "An eye for an eye leaves the whole world blind," "The progress of Mankind," "Let's Party!" We are all a mixed bag. Let's celebrate this and try to find ways to express the multi-storied nature of ourselves in writing. Long live the small story.

Things in life are incomplete, fragmented. The personal essay we just wrote is incomplete. Our relationship with our parents is incomplete. Our understanding of the oceans, or history, or our lover is incomplete, made up of many fragments. And we are incomplete. A truer representation of the real reality of the world acknowledges this. Writing that doesn't try to *hide* the incompleteness is in some way more true to the world than the kind of writing that attempts to tie everything up in a neat bundle.

We often don't *know* what our true intentions are. Ever find, reading your own piece of writing, "Oh, *that's* what I was trying to say"? Read it again in ten years and you'll have a *different* "that's what I was trying to say." Which is true? My answer: Both are true. And if there is no definitive meaning of a piece of writing, that is good. Because then you are free from trying to do something impossible, which is to make *this* piece of writing into something that no one can misunderstand. (I think that the attempt to do so is one of the main reasons so many people speak about writing as so full of suffering: they are trying to do something impossible.)

Thus there is never a final and complete meaning of this world, or of your piece of writing, or of this book, or of why he or she did that. What a joy to let things emerge, and know that even as they do they are never exhausted.

The Secret Order of Hermeneutics and the Text of the World

You, the writer, are a messenger. Hermes was the messenger god. You bring a message. Hermeneutics is a study of how to understand and interpret.

We are the universe creating itself in order to understand itself.

The people who first "did" hermeneutics, long ago, interpreted the Bible. What did God mean? Then, centuries later, people used hermeneutics to interpret the law. What was the intention of the writers of the Constitution? History was then interpreted too. What did it mean, that Russian Revolution? (The meaning changes over time!) Lit-critters also started to interpret. What did Joyce mean?

But what about the text of the world? Of your own life? What does it mean, your parents' divorce? The dream was about a baby moose. What did that mean? Years later she says she never loved you. But back then she said she did. What is the meaning of that? The first time you had sex? Is there a meaning in that? (Let us not look for a One Answer.)

The things that happened yesterday slip away. This causes us sorrow. We lose what has been handed down to us, our Gramma's stories. We lose the conversations, the places, the feelings of ten years ago. The flow of time carries them away. New things come on and on and we become alienated from all that has come before. Writing is some kind of cry in the night against this.

Writing helps us take hold of things, but it doesn't lock them; it is their nature to move. The Buddha said it is vain to try to hold them, but still we feel we must. We love this world. Writing discovers some meanings, and preserves them. But also it changes them. Writing interacts us with these stories, and holds the alienation at bay. It is noble and good to fight back against alienation.

We write to understand. Thus we should write. But we can never fully understand. The world is shifting, and we are shifting under it. Thus we should keep writing.

... a series of approximations toward an ever-changing goal
—Claude Whitmyer

Once, long ago, the hermeneutics people said that if we peel back the layers, the sedimented, encrusted tradition, we can get to what the Buddha really meant. The hermeneutics people today say that this is forever impossible. The past is a foreign country. We are finite: the world is huge, and forever. We can never understand. Still, we try. But how, knowing that we cannot know?

THE SECRET ORDER OF HERMENEUTICS ✦ 235
AND THE TEXT OF THE WORLD

One way: "the hermeneutic circle." Many of the experiments and techniques in this book play with the hermeneutic circle. It's a cycle of investigation, a trying to know. Here's how you do it: We never start from nothing. We ask a question from what we know. "Why do men do that to women?" We start with some understanding of "men," of "women," and what "do that" is, and we fling our question at the world, with our thought, with our pen. The writing itself, and the world, fling back their answers, which shows us the inadequacy of our question, or of our view of "men," "women," or "that." These answers we get (in our writing) revise our questions, and we ask again: again we fling ourselves at the world. Again and again. Will we ever perfectly know? No. However, we try. This is the hermeneutic circle. It's what you've been doing in this book.

When we ask the questions in our writing in a way that replicates the complexity of the world, the questions are better questions. That's why the writing experiments here try to replicate the complexity of this very world.

This writing we do is also making ourselves, and because we act based on what we know, it is making the world. We want to know how to care for the kids, we want to know how to deal with our grief, we want to know how to describe that Taxi ride to the carnival in Lima, Peru. The answers to our questions are based on the view of the world of our dad and mom and the Tonight Show and that Robert Frost poem and our lover's words and everything else that has been poured into our soul. As well as what we bring.

We ourselves are now the revisions of this world. The more open the mind, the more true the understanding, the more wise the action. Let us be the most real and true to life that we can be, revising and revisiting ourselves again and again.

Is This "Writing Open the Mind" Stuff Therapy?

Well . . . one of the great teachings of the Buddha is that awareness and perception will bring you some peace. So to the extent that you do remove the bits and halters from yourself, and encourage reflection, yes, this work can help in the quest to be well. Is that my purpose in this work and this book? Hmmm . . . it's not something I'm against. And yes, in my own experience, the transmutations of what I thought was "reality"—through the juxtaposing and swaying and improvising through the body—has taught me great things, things that help me to be well. But that doesn't mean that's been my purpose in writing this book or doing this work, or that yours has to be. Let's not limit writing in any way at all. Write for fun. Write for knowledge. Write to entertain. Write to explain your life. Write to understand your life. Write to connect to another person. Write just to write. Write because you have no idea why. Or you can write to be well. Everything is OK; let's not predetermine the ends, one way or the other.

Getting "Better" at Writing: Following the Wisp of Smoke Coming Out of the Forest

Following the wisp of smoke that is coming out of the forest: this is, I propose to you, how you will "learn how to write." Learn how to write "better." The wisp is not a bonfire. Not a brush fire. More like a coil of incense smoke caught in the late afternoon sunlight, coming out from between the last trees at the edge of the wood, the light slanting through it, illuminating it, holy, instantaneous. That kind of wisp of smoke.

And this means discovering the way *you uniquely* can use language and put together ideas, how you can use your strong suits, can tap into your own internal fertile crescents. For if you can reliably, or at least more and more over time, touch these sumptuous inner regions, and pull language through and from and out of them, then you will be writing something that not only touches and pleases you again and again when you read it (and pleases you as you write it) but also pleases congruent inner places in others.

In all "others"? No. At all times? No. Will it be "better" by someone's standards (an expert)? Maybe, maybe not. But if you trust the universe (and you should), it's likely that the work coming from that place in you will find its way to a place like that in another person. And more reliably so than if you write from a bunch of two-dimensional *ideas* about proper writing. (And, guess what, you'll also suffer less in writing it if you touch that inner congruence.)

What you do is scatter your seeds out to the wind, and if they're good seeds, and they've been full of what it is that you essentially are, or parts of that, then those seeds will find the places where they germinate and grow. Some will fall on the desert sands or the New Hampshire granite, but even those may someday find their nesting place. The lord moves in mysterious ways.

So what about the wisp of smoke emanating from the forest then?

Here it is. How do you find that fertile true place? It's a feeling, isn't it? Not *word* for a feeling like "Happy" or "Disgruntled," but a sense of something exact and indefinable, something textured and with a certain shape and speed and viscosity. When you know it, you reach in there time and time again, and even though it's shifting, you have a sense that you are in touch with this place, or at least standing in its presence. That place will produce writing in congruence with *you*. And that place of congruence (because you are part of the universe) must by definition touch places in other people, places that will work on them, that will work for them, that will please them, and they will feel the gift of your labors, of your journeys, and they, some of them, in some ways, will respond with that inarticulate and imprecise language of "It is good."

And the wisp of smoke?

> Pay attention to what you pay attention to.
> —David Bayles and Ted Orland

OK, here it is. Write. Write a lot. Write any which way. Produce words. *Keep the pen moving.* That's the first part. It is the prerequisite. When you have a lot of words, read them. You can read them to yourself or you can read them to another. If you are reading them to someone else, tell them that you don't want them to fix or suggest or critique. That would be the end of things. Say it several times if they're not a good listener.

So read it out loud, slowly, and without excuse, explanation, or apology. What you want from your friend, or what you ask yourself to do, is to reflect back to you what she remembers from the piece. Anything at all. Stay away from "I liked it, didn't like it, got confused," etc., just what she remembered, what she responded to.

Now here's the wispy part, the mystical magical dreamy part. Excellent: What you do, as you listen to what she says, is go back in time, in your memory, to the moment *just before you wrote that phrase* (and that's why we want to read the work soon after it was penned) and feel that exact feeling. What was the exact shape and texture and form of this feeling, what words were jittering along in the head, what sense, what intuition, what lack, what inner direction did you give yourself? The effort to go back into the mangrove forest of the mind, the swamp, the woods, and find the place that created that startling phrase—that is what will do more for your writing than anything else. Especially if you go back to it again and again.

Once you do this a few times, you will easily find a little trail back into that luscious grove where the light shines luminous on the tall grasses and the wildflowers in the clearing. You can go there when you want to. Try the process a few more times, and you can shloop! right there in an instant. You see now why you don't want to evaluate it as you go? You see why you don't want your friend to try and fix it for you? You see why you don't want to cloud the listener's mind with what you hoped to try and accomplish, or why you aren't quite happy with it yet? Any of those things startles the process; any of those things breaks the trance necessary; any of those things frightens off the gentle and sensitive forest creature without whom you cannot find the way inside.

Then what happens? What is the demonstrable, weighable, and measurable result? The writing becomes fuller, as a percentage, becomes more saturated with the kind of wording, the kind of insights, the kind of intention that come from this glade in the middle of the woods. It rings true more than the stuff that came from the fixer. It finds its way home.

The Gaggle of People Whose Excellence Courses through These Pages
(Also Known As "Acknowledgments")

My mentor, Claude Whitmyer, once said, "Every book is written by a group of people." Ain't that the truth! Here are those people. First of all, nothing, nothing could have happened without the deep love and steady, hambone-soup strength of Cynthia Kingsbury. From close edits of this book to patches on my psyche and a relentless belief in this work, she is the "that without which not." Next the thanks go to my students, who taught me how all this hocus-pocus works. Anyone who gets something from this book is indebted to them for their years of support.

A powerful gratitude goes to two mentors and guides, Susan Mathews-Scott, "the Sufi master teaching at the back of the carpet shop," and Claude Whitmyer, an exquisite craftsman of life work. Incantations also to Adam Kinsey who talked writing mystery and kaballa into my ears for over a decade. I thank also my teachers, Leslie Kirk Campbell of Ripe Fruit, and the incandescent philosopher-queens of teaching writing at the English composition program at San Francisco State, Catharine Lucas and Jo Keroes. Gracious thanks to Edith Couturier and Jean Jaques Couturier, my mother and father, who poured into my young ears their love of the unusual and fun in language (as well as their disrespect for authority). This book very much wouldn't be in your hands without one Ashley Chase, acquisitions editor at Ulysses Press, who pulled a tab off a poster ("Writing from the Subconscious"?!) stapled to a telephone pole, and wrote me an email. The look and the very readability of this book is due to the above-and-beyond labors of my editor, Lynette Ubois.

I wish also to thank the sensory cavalcade of the country of India, the mystery of Japan, and the exuberance of West Africa, without which this book could not be what it is. Also, amazement is offered to the phenomenon of John Chung, who knows the body is never a blunt instrument. Gratitude also to John Gibler, who said, "Madness! Start Writing!" And to my cousin and life-long pal Jim Boorsten, who, in between walking the perimeter of Manhattan and restoring the Dakota, insisted that I write such a book, and thus, in the flux of universe-energy, caused it to happen. A witchingly deep gratitude also to Chris Twemlow, who spoke gorgeously on the phenomenology *and* hermeneutics of the holy spirit. Also to my brother and poet John Couturier who has been telling me "It's OK" for my whole damn life.

I also give Jah all the thanks and praises for Felix Rentschler who in a teenage attic hangout helped me connect to the delicious flavorings of syllable sounds. I thank also Kim Sevcik, for her lucidity and care, Krista Hiser for her sterling and potent takes on writing and teaching, Julie Sparling, dramatiste, Aimee Ginsberg who said, "Of *course* you can do it!" Nadine Rambeau who said, "Dude, don't you have any more exercises?" Greg Couturier for the drawing he gave to this book at my eleventh hour, and the people of the Bay Area Writing Project who started me out on this journey of teaching writing. Lastly, I'd like to dedicate part of this effort to the memory of Mike Pelton, one of the most helpful and considerate persons that there's ever been.

May this book be a conduit for some of the good things in this life that all these people have given me.

Other Books from Ulysses Press

1001 LITTLE HEALTH MIRACLES
Esme Floyd, $12.95
A treasure trove of friendly health tips that offer shortcuts to feeling good, looking great and living healthy.

A CHORUS OF WISDOM
Edited by Sorah Dubitsky   Foreword by Stephen and Ondrea Levine, $14.95
Essays from over 25 visionary thinkers that offer insight and revelation in a manner that is sure to bring positive change.

COURAGE AFTER FIRE: COPING STRATEGIES FOR RETURNING SOLDIERS AND THEIR FAMILIES
Keith Armstrong, L.C.S.W., Dr. Paula Domenici and Dr. Suzanne Best, $14.95
Provides a comprehensive guide to dealing with the all-too-common repercussions of combat duty, including posttraumatic stress symptoms, anxiety, depression and substance abuse.

HOW MEDITATION HEALS: A SCIENTIFIC EXPLANATION
Eric Harrison, $12.95
In straightforward, practical terms, *How Meditation Heals* reveals how and why meditation improves the natural functioning of the human body.

ONE SOUL, MANY LIVES: FIRST-HAND STORIES OF REINCARNATION AND THE STRIKING EVIDENCE OF PAST LIVES
Roy Stemman, $12.95
This remarkable collection of true stories brings together an impressive body of physical evidence and fascinating accounts of reincarnation.

SECRETS OF THE PEOPLE WHISPERER: A HORSE WHISPERER'S TECHNIQUES FOR ENHANCING COMMUNICATION AND BUILDING RELATIONSHIPS

Perry Wood, $12.95

Presents "horse whisperer" principles as powerful tools for connecting with people on every level: mentally, verbally, physically and spiritually.

STOP LIVING YOUR JOB, START LIVING YOUR LIFE: 85 SIMPLE STRATEGIES TO ACHIEVE WORK/LIFE BALANCE

Andrea Molloy, $12.95

A successful personal life coach shows how to identify priorities, make meaningful decisions and take specific actions.

JOURNEY TO TIBET'S LOST LAMA: A WOMAN'S PILGRIMAGE, THE KARMAPA IN EXILE AND THE FATE OF MODERN TIBET

Gaby Naher, $14.95

A personal, spiritual and historical journey to the exiled 17th Karmapa and into the fascinating culture of Tibet and its Lama heritage.

To order these books call 800-377-2542 or 510-601-8301, fax 510-601-8307, e-mail ulysses@ulyssespress.com, or write to Ulysses Press, P.O. Box 3440, Berkeley, CA 94703. All retail orders are shipped free of charge. California residents must include sales tax. Allow two to three weeks for delivery.

About the Author

Essayist, poet, and writing teacher Andy Couturier is the director of The Opening (www.theopening.org), a center for courses in writing in Oakland, California. He is a student of

 improvisational theater and Buddhist meditation, and has induced altered states with such consciousness-bending experiences as hitchhiking across the Sahara desert and guiding Japanese tourists (in Japanese) through the sites of San Francisco. He has a master's degree in teaching writing, and he has written for newspapers, magazines, and literary journals, including *The Japan Times*, *Adbusters*, *Creative Non-Fiction*, and *The North American Review*. He has lived in India, West Africa, and Japan, and has been teaching the techniques in this book for over a decade. One of his essays was recently nominated for a Pushcart Prize.